I0456146

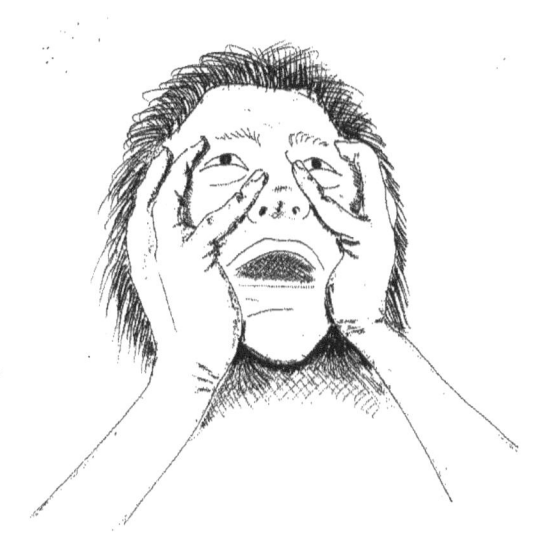

God save me.
I need water,,, food,,,
A home,

a car, a job, a new TV, microwave and
a waffle iron, and,,,

1

Each of us,,, every man woman and child is responsible for the outcome facing us, as Mother Nature is about to enact **Nature's Rights** regardless of the gods.

GOD

is **NOT** going to help save us from what man has done to the earth.

God helps those that help themselves,,, and I don't mean to all the money.

There is not a lot of time left.

Natures Rights

Sequel of
Global Financial Super Heating
2014

Written and Illustrated by

William J. Ryan

Nature's Rights

--- First Edition ---

The thing is most of us know it is going to happen,,, we just don't know when. What will bring down the systems that support us all? All those unseen systems that keep at bay primitive life that most of all of us know nothing about.

This book explores what will happen, how, when, where and most important what will the future look like? How can you prepare for a disastrous future if you have no idea what it is going to look like?

Knowledge is the key to surviving what is to come. If you do not understand, you can never be prepared for what is just on the door step waiting for you.

It is not a matter of if,,, it is a matter of when.

When we all turn a blind eye to the destructive events going on around us, and use religion as justification to murder other people that we employed, it is called Scrupulosity.

It is the **insanity** found within all religions.

Scrupulosity:
I detailed the insanity found in all religions and broke it down into four parts in a book called;

Scrupulosity

You can buy the book Scrupulosity at Amazon.com in both paperback and on Kindle

About The Author

You, the reader, should know that I am an autodidact (self-directed learner) and I am dyslexic and not only suffer from letters, numbers and spelling of words changing on me, but structuring of sentences will sometimes be backwards.

Because this book is fact based, as I presently know them, I made many discoveries along the way that opened up my mind to our future, and any way I look at it,,, **it's not good**. That will be hard for some of you to read,,, but read it and I hope it will prepare you for what I think will be coming at us all **very soon**.

Things are moving at us very fast and in all the wrong directions. In the past 100 years we have created a future that is very bleak and all but destroyed any hope for man. I would not have thought one race of beings could consume so much in the race to gain the pretense of value,,, the almighty **god/note**.

Forward

"What the hell is going on?"

In this book I make an attempt to talk about what no one is willing to talk about. That is what is facing us all within the coming years,,, the 6th Die Off.

In my book **Global Financial Super Heating**, I talked of the future of life on the planet when the paper currency collapse's... and it will collapse. This book will examine the future of the millennium children and what life will be like for them and their decedents,,, the next 4 generations.

It is about the conversion of the planet's atmosphere, from clean breathable air to toxic gas, via unregulated human population growth, causing the cutting down of the forest in order to grow food. Also, it's about the burning of fossil fuels, creating carbon dioxide and carbon monoxide (air conversion).

We all are entering new territories the planet has never seen. One thing is clear and that is we have less and less breathable air and less and less drinkable water. Both of which are requirements to sustain life for we humans.

The following drawing shows the thin blue space in which we all live and because we all live within a fluid environment, this level changes as the winds blow. In the past, it has been estimated the troposphere ranged in height of 30,000 feet to 56,000 feet. The dotted line shows the reduction or **Atmospheric Consumption** of breathable air over the past 100 years. Now that should disturb any of you that are paying attention, for that is a lot of air in a very short amount of time.

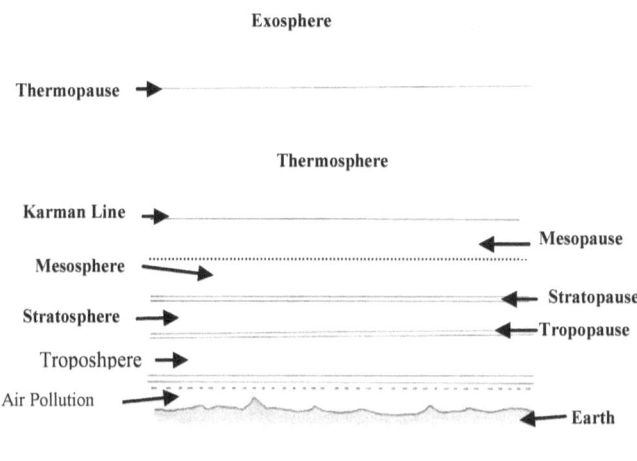

Chart One

One example of this recent reduction of the planet's atmosphere or what I call **Atmospheric Consumption** is proven by the lowering of the **Winds Aloft**. Our planet's atmosphere is made up of no less than ten levels and you see one of them every day and probably don't even know what you are looking at.

1. **Troposphere**: that thin space in which we all live and all known life resides within the universe.
2. **Tropopause:** thin space between
3. **Stratosphere**: the layer of the earth's atmosphere above the troposphere.
4. **Ozone layer:** waving in at around 49,000 to 110,000 feet.
5. **Stratopause:** thin space between was about 170,000 feet.
6. **Mesosphere:** the region of the atmosphere between the stratosphere and thermosphere.
7. **Mesopause:** once topped out at around 260,000 to 280,000 feet.
8. **Karman Line:** was 330,000 feet.
9. **Thermosphere:** About 50 miles above the earth's surface.
10. **Thermopause**: at one time was 1,100,000 to 2,600,000 feet.
11. **Exosphere**: topping off the planet's atmosphere at a waving height of between 1,700,000 to 3,300.000.

The spinning planet pulls at the air particles dragging them along the surface causing air currents. It took 100s of millions of years for all the plants to make the air we all breathe and we are burning through good air in just over 100 years. Because of the action of the planets spinning, I can only approximate the reduction of the Troposphere at between 8,000 to 10,000 feet. (See dotted line in **Chart One** on page 10)

The Troposphere is broken apart into layers of 5,000 feet in the next drawing. This shows the first layer we see when looking up at the clouds. It is that flat part where evaporation of water starts to break through and accumulate.

Chart Two

The proven recent reduction of this planet's overall atmosphere, or what I call **Atmospheric Consumption**, is found within the reduction of hurricanes and their severity. Now this is one of those things the government will not talk about, but this is very important and proves my point. The following drawing (**Chart Three**) shows a normal hurricane and its highest as it has grown in the past atmosphere. Some of these storms were massive in size and had devastating effects on shipping and land.

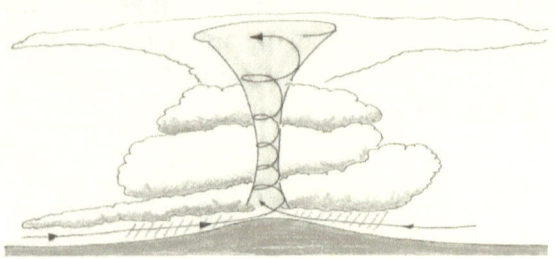

Chart Three

Recent news accounts still show named hurricanes, however those storms are not as strong as in the past and the numbers are less than expected and predicted. *Now I am talking in just the past 10 to 20 years.*

The dis-information presented for our consumption by the government controlled new media, tells us these new and developing storms "will not develop due to **Wind Shearing**". It is my understanding that the term **Wind Shearing** is what planes run into when flying and when they are trying to land, as the upper level of very thin air or the **Stratosphere** comes crashing down into the **Troposphere**.

News reports also show more planes seem to be running into this turbulence, regardless of all the new types of radar and computers that can predict these and help to avoid them. See **Chart Four**. The new turbulence is caused by the **Atmospheric Consumption** and conversion to toxins. Less lower air, more turbulent thinner air.

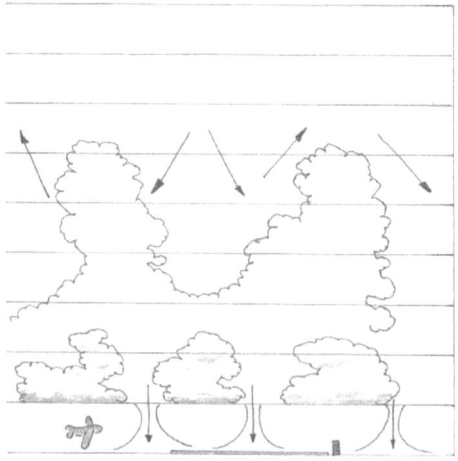

Chart Four

The term **Wind Shearing** is a misleading terms being fed to us, and is not 100% factual; as to the actions taking place in the **Troposphere**. The **Atmospheric Consumption** is converting air into toxic gas and as thicker breathable air is converted, the level of good air is lowered and contaminated. What the weather man tells us is, **"Wind Shearing"** is in fact, **Upper Atmosphere Severing** or **U.A.S.**

Hurricanes are today having their tops cut away and not permitted to gain in strength to the levels in the past, because there is **less air**. It has been converted into Carbon Dioxide, Carbon Monoxide and other toxins,,, all within the past 100 years.

This trend will continue until the crash of global currencies occur, causing mass starvation and migration of the masses. The following illustration **Chart Five** shows how hurricanes cannot develop, as **Upper Atmosphere Severing (U.A.S.)** continues its relentless path upon the earth and we who live upon it.

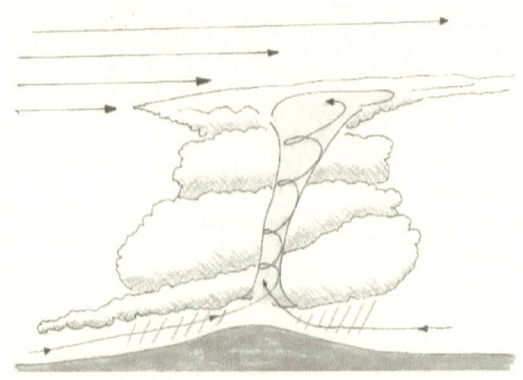

Chart Five

The future holds for us all, a continued reduction of breathable air converted into toxic gas at an accelerated rate. The planet is entering new ground, as each of the next 4 millennium generations move into the future. The following chart shows how carbon dioxide is on a straight line up.

Please note,,, up is toxic levels not seen on the earth in millions of years,,, new man made ground.

Carbon Dioxide Atmospheric Chart
An accumulation of mutable studies assembled in approximate values to show only future values.

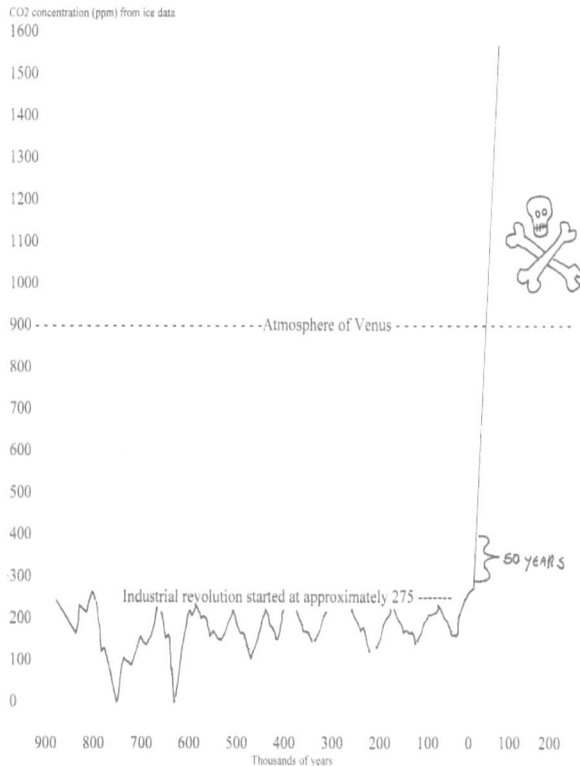

William J. Ryan ©2014 #038

Chart Six

The following chart shows a reduction in air as the quality is ever reduced and each of us must draw into our lungs man made airborne toxin. At this rate, the **Troposphere** will be mostly used up, as these toxins are dumped into the seas killing off that life as well.

Chart Seven

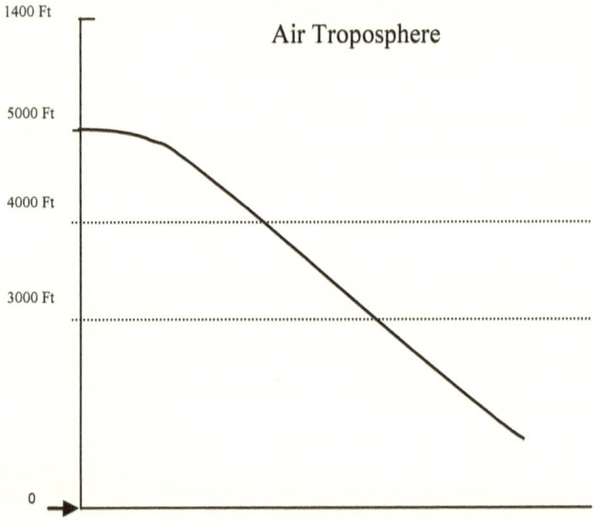

Air Troposphere

Burying your heads in denial,,, Ignoring the truth,,, ignoring facts,,, ignoring reality,,, placing this all upon the gods shoulders,,, is not going to change the outcome and the future that is facing all of us.

Images

The first page of this book sums up my view of how most people look upon life,,, **internally**,,, the gift that they have collectively received and are wasting. My view of most people is that they do not want to look at the future; for they can already see it. **You know what is coming... You choose not to look... because you are weak, helpless and terrified! You depend on God to fix it all.**

The second image (page 17) is how people protect themselves from the reality that is all around them. Whenever they should find themselves looking too hard at the future, they must look the other way or bury their heads in the sand and not look at all. They think, *'I don't want to listen to the negative people because they are not saying what we want to hear.'* These people just don't want to know the truth.

The following pages are to be as condensed as I can make them and still be able to convey the point that the planet earth is crashing into reality like a freight train into a goat-drawn wagon full of watermelons (us). The end result will be the same, total destruction of all (or most) life. **And no one wants to look at the train. It is coming hard and it is coming fast!!!**

It is not that people are stupid and could never understand,,, no it's not that. It is that they don't want to understand, for it will not make them

happy and they must be happy. It will not make them rich or bring them things, and they must have all the newest things,,, the self absorbed, small minded, superior to everyone else, the
Gadget People.

Joy trumps reality every time.

Happiness and joy are not to be found within these pages,,, only my attempt to look forward into the devastation that is reality, coming at us very fast.

Nature's Rights

1. How are you to prepare?
2. Where is it best for you to live?
3. What will replace air?
4. Where will there be food?
5. Where will there be water?
6. What will you use for money?
7. How do you avoid the FEMA death camps?
8. How do you avoid the mass starvation of the future?
9. How do you protect yourself from the collapse of the global **god/note** that will start the mass migration of the starving, willing to kill you and take what you have because they did not prepare?

If you're not up to it, then don't read on,,, and the ones that do will most likely have a better chance of survival.

Nature's Rights

Chapter One
Government, Patents and Traitors
Patents 38
Women's Rights 51
Martial Law 54
Gun Bans 61
Stuxnet 64

Chapter Two
Money, Gold, Silver and Tangibles
Robots Take Human Jobs 71
Human or Computer 73
Selling Baby Parts 76
Gold and Silver 80
Money or the God/Note 82
Orchestrated Devaluation 86
Military Payment Certificate 92

Chapter Three
Weather and the Environment
Warm Blob 100
Straw Houses 107
Sand Mafia 109
Coastal Erosion 112
Godzilla Weather Patterns 114
Hurricanes 115
Global Weather
changes and Droughts 117
The Bottom Half 122

Chapter Four
Air
Chemicals in Our Homes 134
Radiation 135

Chapter Five
    Global Shading
        Space Sun Shade 146
Chapter Six
    Water,,,, Juice Of The Stars
        Sinkholes 157
        The Black Sea 158
        Polar Ice Melting 159
        Drinking Water
        Contamination 163
        Forest Fire Chemicals 167
        Oceanic Garbage 169
        Plastic Beach in Hawaii 170
        Rare Earth Elements
        Sea Gypsies 171
Chapter Seven
    Starvation
        German Flower Building 180
        German and England White
        Movement 182
        God and Papal Supremacy 184
        1300 187
        Food and Weed Control 189
        Horse Meat for Human Consumption
        Water is Food 198
        Aquifers' Other Purpose 202
Chapter Eight
    Martial Law FEMA Death Camps
        Bill of Attainder 213
        Death Camps 214
        Citizens Commission to Investigate
        the FBI 215
        Cointelpro 217

Nature's Rights

Debtors Prison 218
Sovereign Citizen Movement ... 218
Letters to Congress 219
Libya 221
The Terracotta Army 222

Chapter Nine
  Pandemics
Doomsday Clock 228
COTE Calendar 229
Zoos 230
Superbugs 231
  The Big Three
Governments 232

Chapter Ten
  The Point of No Return
What is to come? 246
Water 247
Food 248
Air   ....
249

Global Warming 250
The Solution 252
Cannibalism 253
Defense of One's Castle 256
Coin of the Realm 257
Silver 258

Dictionary 313
Other Books 320

Nature's Rights

Chapter One

Religions,
De- Education
Governments,
Patents
& Traitors

**Massive government building,,,
anywhere in the world.**

This first chapter is to cover many subjects and topics that individually offer some evidence of an underlying effort to change and control the world by the few. However, collectively these examples help point to the direction society is heading as Nature prepares for disaster (DEATH) on a biblical scale.

I have provided charts (some with dates) to show the fast decline we are all on, entering the 6th Die Off. However, most of us just can't see the future because of all the confusing information and **misinformation** being deliberately fed to us. In my attempt to ferret out the truth from the fiction, some of the available information known to me at this time may not be 100% accurate, due to planted and misleading information. For the many subjects covered in this book and the presumptions I have made, I ask you to look at the overall information with an open mind, for it all leads in one direction.

The disturbing facts are that all charts point in one direction, and that is a time when the inevitable collapse of all societies will occur.

Each chart has its own timeline; so I have merged each time to create a single date and time, in order to find the elusive, collective time of the point of no return, in front of us all. The beginnings of the 6th Die Off facing man.

We all know it is coming,,, we just don't know when. Worse than the date is; how will we survive if our eyes are closed? How will your children live in a world ill prepared for mass starvation and the failure of the global god/notes? The question should be for all of us,,, What is the Finish date; the date when all life as we know it is over.

All of us know,,, all of us can see,,, the death spiral has started,,, as we blindly observe Nature's Rights kill off an infection,,, an invasion a parasite upon its skin,,, us.

Parasite

The illusion of democracy is for the most part, to most of us, nothing more than the freedom of the rich to **take money** (wealth **god/notes**) from the poor (the rest of us). Or the freedom to create the poor out of hard working people with laws such as, **'you must buy insurance,,, (that will never pay a claim),,, IT'S THE LAW.'** Try to remember,,, these titans of industry cannot control people if they are educated and understand.

Governments (or those that run religion and governments, the string masters) have learned long ago that it is necessary to force **religion** on the masses,,, to help control them (as history has shown us). Therefore, religion (god,,, any god will do) is a must in a so called 'free market system', so the ones at the helm, (many hands on the wheel), can suppress the ones pushing the ship of state (the poor). The illusion of democracy (we all have a say) must prevail via one religion, while stomping out all descending voices (wrong religion or no religion). *It is how they control the masses and ultimately... the money* (god/notes).

Today, there can be little doubt that we live within one **type of Theocracy** (a form of government where the clergy have sovereignty over people and territory) and the outcome will be the same as it has been in the past. The **Muslim Brotherhood** launched a political party **in the United States** as of April 7, 2014 with an eye on the 2016 elections. This is the same thing as the Christian parties (republican – democrat) we have in America now. Where their religion (Catholic,

Christian, protestant, Etc.), is being forced on the rest of us, separated by the Jew's.

Regardless of the religion, time is running out and **Nature's Rights** will soon be forced upon all of us. Suppression of the truth is their only option, for they are committed.

Examples;

March 24, 2016

Based upon religion, new laws are now crossing the country at disturbing speeds. North Carolina just wrote a law permitting discrimination against all gays and transgender people (based on religion). If we do not rise up against this religious influence, ISIS will come here and pass laws permitting the murder of all Christians and other infidels. It's at our door step,,, it is at our feet.

The first amendment to the Constitution of the United States reads; *"Congress shall make no law respecting an establishment of religion, or prohibiting the free exercise thereof,,,"* For most of us this is the **Separation of Church and State** concept being suppressed. However, if we permit one religion to take over,,, suppression and murder is what you will get, as we see crossing the globe today. They have done it before,,, are doing it now,,, and will do it in the future enriching themselves all the way. Pretending it is not happening does not work.

The religious wars fought by the religious theocracy powers across the globe have been waged too enrich the few. War pays well for the few and religion is the best way to start an enriching war. Religion is the best distraction for the masses (justification) as they (the string masters), the rich, enrich themselves on the holly,,, whatever religious side you are on.

Now a new religion has learned from the Christians how to take over and they are coming at us with a vengeance. More distractions to take our eye off of the disaster, **Nature's Rights** that is coming our way and very,,, very soon.

Education within any government is not to be tolerated (by the few) for any government, Communism, Socialism or a free market system of freely elected leaders is 100% corruptible. *Absolute power corrupts absolutely. Who has the power to buy each government regardless of and because of theologies?* Those people of super money handpick ($$$) our leaders and use religion.

So if it is not a Theocracy where the super money people believe in god, then it can only be some type of **Autocracy**, (supreme power is concentrated in the hands of one person) and now it starts to make sense. But who are these people and what power do they control that can take over the worlds governments,,, and why?

It would seem the worst of the worst gravitate to these positions, like pedophiles gravitate to the Roman Catholic Church; each will protect their own, regardless of the atrocities committed. *As long as all of us say and do nothing,,, or chose to remain ignorant,,, they commit war crimes enriching themselves.* ***You must overcome these stumbling blocks.***

Reasoning and higher education (understanding how the planet and life works) is needed to replace the greedy hands at the wheel as the years move on; but the lower underlings, the ones that push the ship, the **Goyim**,,, are not to be educated,,, and in my estimation, de-education is the plan and I believe it is to late. *For we all have passed the tipping point of no return.*

It is the reason that over the past 100 years in America, the education system has lowered the bar for graduation of high school. There are many that made it through the 12th grade, have their diploma and can't read it. *How does this make America stronger,,, it does not,,, it makes the ones that control America stronger via this de-education system... the pretence of an education system stronger and richer.*

In America today most of the school systems have some of the best facilities in the world and yet, we are on the way down the ladder of success in the world as to the level of education coming from these new state of the art facilities. Some reports, (and there are many) place America in the world at 28th from the top, in math and science.

This new **Common Core State Standards** provides our young students with the skills of how to pass a test. But this is not new, when I got out of high school the only thing as to preparing me for life was, I walked away with the knowledge of how to write a check." The education plan of useless information making you controllable,,, de-educated is not new.

When I was a kid going through the system, just as I was understanding math, they changed the system. We received new books, mid-year, on how to learn math and even the teacher did not understand. It made no sense and I don't think I could have passed if the teacher hadn't given me the answers,,, as they do today. Forty years later, I hear we are introducing "New Math" once more and shoving it down our kids' throats.

The new math curriculum reportedly is "far outside the student's ordinary experiences," "puts new demands on teachers" and would only benefit the writers and book manufacturers and of course the ones behind government pulling the strings (read more on these people in my book, *Deceivers*). *This shows a deliberate pattern of de-education built within the system. The beneficiaries are those above the government pulling the strings. Look up and behind your leaders,,, if you are ever to understand.*

This one example (math) shows me, it is not quality the government is looking for but de-education of the masses is the primary goal. For their disingenuous attempts to improve the system of education for expedience did not work 40 years ago and will not achieve anything but confusion again (the plan). That is the goal, the true goal of a theocracy or autocracy government,,, **for you cannot control educated people**,,, you must keep them ignorant and religious. *That is the underlying goal of either type of government in place,,, Theocracy or Autocracy.*

March 19, 2015

India; 'Students caught cheating on exams.' This report shows parents climbing outside three story walls to give their kids inside the answers to the tests so they can pass. These images show almost each window of this large building has someone's mom or dad passing notes with the answers to the students. When I saw that, I wondered about the Indian doctors coming to this country. *This clearly shows,,, the value is in the paper diploma,,, not in the knowledge.*

Asia is kicking our butts in education. It could be that they put such importance on knowledge for their people as a whole. A race of people wanting a better life and they know it is done one way,,, hard work. ***True education.***

To me this education thing is not hard. I received much knowledge from dead people (books, tapes) and now that we have the ability to record the best, we only have to play that recording to all students. When we find the best we can keep using them to teach from beyond the grave.

This DUM-ification of the masses is done for the benefit of the very few. The ones at the top of the top (#1) of the list are the super, super rich, Kings, Lords, Gods, Religions (of the past), Financial Empires,,, the Money-Gods,,, old money.

Next up (#2) is power,,, oil, wind, water, sun, electricity, ensure those in power remain in power, so they position themselves in such a manner that they (#1) own or control (#2). They are hand in hand and always move together for neither can, or will, ever stand alone. *Money and power,,, use religion,,, to control the de-educated.*

There are two more that support (#1) and (#2) and give them the power and wealth to protect and ensure their dynasties. (#3) is the military of each country and (#4) is god and religion (not as powerful as before) blind faith. For we (the masses, the Goyim) blindly and ignorantly step into both these slots (religion, military) created and controlled by the power and the money (**god/notes**) created by (#1).

This same formula is used all over the earth and regardless of the government (religion), this system always remains the same. Whatever the ideologies (theocracy), the outcome remains the same,,, total destruction of all resources, life and then the planet. *That is the future before us all, for blindly stepping into line, following our bought and paid for leaders,,, the faces of governments,,, owned by #1.*

We all know this to some degree or can see one part of this whole system, but just don't have the time or take the time or create the time to look,,, because we just don't want to see. People know in their hearts that the end is coming and would rather bury their heads in the sand, hiding from the truth where it is safe and free from the reality of the future and all that is to come, because of their ignorance. Bought and paid for by the masters, the lords, kings, Theocracy, Autocracy and oh yes,,, the gods and their religion,,, with all its ignorance,,, owned by #1.

The first thing that you must do is stop being gullible, then <u>stop speed reading</u>. You have been trained to believe you can absorb needed information by skimming. It is not true,,, you must slow down and absorb each word and its meaning. The de-educators will tell you that skimming is how to pass the test,,, this (life) is not a test and if it were, most are failing it,,, badly.

STOP SPEED READING!!!

The information found within these pages is grim at best,,, but you must look at it to see into the future and position yourself, your family, for what we know is coming. **The ringing of Mother Nature's death bell** is becoming deafening and only if you pull your head out of you're a— you will hear it and you will see what is to come. For the **Death knell** lies just before us and we stand on the precipice of Mother Nature's calculated end of humanity. *She is so close, coming up behind you. Can't you hear her steps coming?* **Nature's Rights** *will prevail most dramatically and very soon.*

The question is not if,,, but when? How will the known end to come,,, come and what will it look like? How will I,,, how can I and my family survive? The first trick is to know the coming **date** of no return,,, or have we passed it. That **time** when we cross it,,, the tipping point,,, there is no going back to fix it. There is no recovery from what we have done for the sake of God and the almighty **god/notes**.

The full price of permitting the planets resources to be exploited is but one part of Nature's Rights to withdraw life and start over. If man is to survive at all,,, then where,,, how?

I personally believe we have passed that date of no return, and the tipping point was in the 80's when there was still a lot of good air. The point of mass starvation across the globe and wave of the mass exodus of the starving heading our way is next up,,, but when?

The answer to those questions and more is what I am trying to cover in these pages. I am trying to pull the facts, as I know them, as I find them,,, together. But it should be known that the power (#1) is to rewrite history at every turn and it is at this point removing images,,, re-writing history,,, that will better control the masses,,, we Goyim.

Most all people I speak to know "it's" coming and coming fast,,, but what is "it"? When will "it" get here and what will "it" look like? How will "it" unfold before our eyes and what will life be like for each of us after "it" happens?

Recap

Theocracy – Autocracy

(#1)   the one at the top and the super, super rich, controlled by the Deceivers, the String Masters.

(#2)   oil, power, water, nuclear, money

(#3)   all military

(#4)   god, religions

Where do I start? The Deceivers running this planet have created so many lies that one man cannot untangle them in his lifetime. One can only do ones best to expose the truth and with that the future for all of us. In no particular order, I start with,,,

Patents

Most people don't have an opportunity to use or enter the criminally corrupt cult, guarded by the rich, of the United States Trademark and Patent Offices, however I have. On more than one occasion I have tried to patent an idea for a new product (over the past 30 years) and run into a wall of such a monumental, complexity, ever growing in size. Today its size would block the sun from view and plunge our earth into total darkness,,, as it is, for America. The dark side has truly taken over.

But why would a government make it harder for a citizen to get protection for an idea that would help the country be financially stronger and help humanity?

The people that work at the patent office in Washington DC are like all politicians,,, **traitors to this country**, loyal to the super rich. We all know politicians have sold us all out for the profits of #1 and the super, super rich. But this is part of what will bring down a nation,,, as it is.

I, like you (most of you), thought the patent office was here to help protect the creative people and their new and inventive ideas,,, (for us in this country) but you would be wrong. **The patent office is full of traitors** and they do everything to stop any one from getting a patent. They don't help,,, but do the opposite,,, hinder every attempt to help America become stronger with new ideas. Guarding and protecting the sacred, almighty, illusive patent.

It is one more reason America is crashing and it is why I placed patents at the front of this book. A country's strength comes from our creative forward looking minds and we all should encourage this on every level. But this sacred government discourages every person and every attempt to better our nation. #1 cannot control you if you build and invent a better system. They can only control the old system. They defend it with the one power they have; money and they buy these people controlling our future and their past wealth.

It has become so expensive and complicated that only the few can circumvent the manmade obstacles and land mines placed in such a way as to enrich patent attorneys and discourage the average

Joe. The end result is, America does not get a new idea that could create jobs and make America stronger as we move forward in time. *The philosophy of the power over the U.S. Patent office (#1) is, 'not invented here' meaning, if the super rich corporations want it, they will invent it,,, all others need not apply.*

Perhaps (and I believe this to be true) the attorney business also wanted to make things so complicated that like most things now you must hire an attorney to do anything. *Attorneys design everything so as to enrich attorneys.* They have over the approximate past 100 years made it so expensive and so compacted that the small guy does not have a chance. Just the way big business, (#1) ($$$) wants it regardless of what the government is saying. (Autocracy)

100 years ago the United States Patent Office would help you get your patent through their office,,, enriching America. Today they do everything they can to stop you; As though Al Qaeda or ISIS were running the Patent Office.

Today it has become so hard (and expensive) to work your way through the patent office, the keepers of the sacred patent numbers, that the patent attorney job opportunities are declining. *That is right,,, declining in an ever growing world. We in America are falling behind because those truly in power want it that way. Why? Traitors to this country are on both sides. The 1%ers want all the patents for themselves so they are the only ones to make money. The attorneys want all the work preventing the small guy (the rest of us) from success and they get your money.*

They (attorneys) have become like the auto mechanics of today's new car stores. Mechanics are leaving the industry because it has become so complicated, deliberately difficult to work on a new car. They tell me they have to pass countless tests from the manufacturer and now have to be an electrical engineer to open the hood of your car. The industry has put them out of work. *Hence; killing the little guy to enrich themselves.*

The only growing sector of the patent attorney market of America I can find is coming from,,, you guessed it,,, another countries. Example; We are making people in India richer by farming out this expensive, American, patent attorney work,,, to foreign countries.

Now stop and think of that,,, we Americans are giving away our best ideas,,, the intricacies of those sparks of brilliance that make America what it is,,, or was. We don't need Al-Qaeda,,, we don't need ISIS,,, we have the United States Patent and Trademark Office and its traitorous employees to bring this country down to its knees,,, as it has done.

I did find the number decline of patent applications; it's a report estimating that from 2008 to 2018 the decline will be approximately 30%. If 2008 is 100% or the best of times and ten years later there is a decline in applications, this is a drop of 3% per year in spite of the American Invents Act.

This information is only relevant to show but one more cause of the crash that is at our door step and how America is declining in other ways you may not have thought of.

Decline of Patents

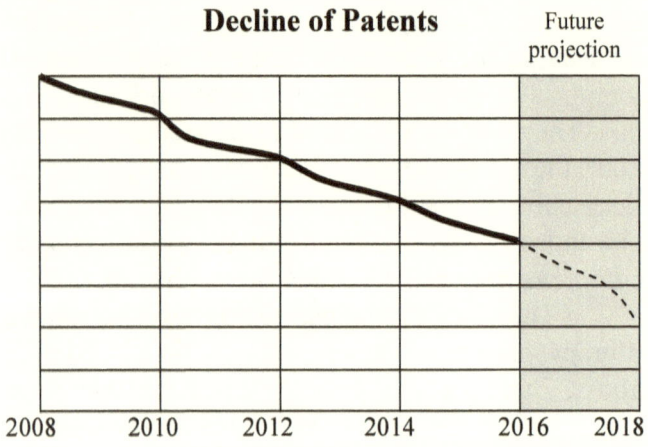

Future projection

To show you just how powerful the one percentor's or power industry (nuclear, oil) are in the world today, look at what they (money, power over governments) are doing. So, I believe the market crash point for patent applications is within the next 5 to 10 years.

August 19, 2015
Taxing the Sun

Spain has an estimated 3,000 hours of sunlight every year and their government has strongly pursued solar development over the past years. At this time it has become one of the top producers of solar energy in the world. That is a good thing,,, right? The only thing is, they are now too good and per the government, are now about

60% exceeding demands. Too much free electricity! Wow!!!

Free electricity is just not a thing even a government can do for its people,,, for its businesses, for its economy and for the environment. Not even a government can make cheaper safer electricity work,,, when it is working. So Spain has to tax and fine people that have solar panels,,, thereby enriching the ones with the wires, (nuclear, oil, coal and #1) power and penalizing the poor.

The following is to provide you with background necessary to understand the declining future before us all.

January 23, 2015

It was reported on this day that the United States (Christian) is now increasing the "Civilian Assistance" amount given to Yemen (Muslim) from 22 million to 307 million,,, American tax dollars not being spent on roads and bridges in America. Some of us believe "Civilian Assistance" means war supplies arming the one side of Muslims so that they could kill each other. *'Let my enemy kill my enemy'*. This disabling action is to some of us revenge for the 1974 oil crisis. But it is much more than that,,, read ***Jesus Christ in Canaan***. Arming newly formed terrorist groups, (Al Qaeda and ISIS) in this way, destabilizes the region so American corporations (American interests) can get the **Arab oil** (money, power) and, like idiots, we all step into line. *We all are authorizing their criminal genocidal actions with our silence.*

Then we send our young, our future, our brightest, to fight and die in this religious crusade to get oil and power; America loses. And if they should make it home missing an arm or leg,,, the American government dumps them like trash on to the street,,, homeless.

It should be noted that ISIS was reportedly formed in 1999, and France states their name also to be *"Daesh,"* from the Arabic words *Daes* (one that crushes something underfoot") or *Dahes* (showing discord.")

February 3, 2015

Reportedly this day should be the end of John Kiriakou (retired CIA agent whistle blower) incarceration for allegedly being the first to have passed classified information to a reporter regarding the **United States (Christian) torturing Muslims** via waterboarding.

Like Snowden and other brave American men, we would not know what this corrupt **Theocracy Autocracy** government was up to, if these brave men did not stand up to this cartel, exposing this for all of us to see. *From where some people sit, he is but one more political prisoner in the American slanted injustice system. The questions are; how many more are there and who will be next?*

March 14, 2015

It was reported that 47 republicans signed a letter to Iran, stating that any nuclear deal made with Democrats would only last as long as these democrats were in office. This letter, some believe, only helps show how unreliable America's word is,,, helping to destabilize the region even more. Iran wisely, knows not to trust America and this is just in your face, America's word is not good. *Please note, this is one religion vs. another,,, controlled by the power people, using religion, enriching war profiteer supplies,,, that's what weapons are made for,,, killing and money from the oil,,, enriching the 1%ers,* but for how much longer?

March 24, 2015

It was reported that the United States and British forces are pulling out of Yemen, aiding and abetting in a failed state, **destabilizing the region**. America first give them money,,, then raise that amount and when Yemen are addicted to American free cash,,, we pull out. We give Yemen war supplies,,, then we pull out leaving them (war supplies) for the newly formed terrorists (Al Qaeda and ISIS) thereby, expanding the destabilization, the war and the need for war supplies.

It should be noted that America and England are Christian and are arming both sides of the Muslim people and country. The deeper plan is 'let my enemy kill my enemy',,, oh yes, and here is the money for corruption and the weapons you will need to kill each other.

Then all the corrupt news industry's report,,, "We just don't know why they want to kill Americans."

April 11, 2015

United Nations Chief states that "Syria resembles a death camp". Russia and America,,, (both Christian),,, on both sides killing Muslims as well as arming Muslims to kill each other. Millions have migrated to get away from this most recent Christian crusade and genocide fleeing to other countries with their hands out begging. *And what do you think their reactions are going to be when they find out American Christians are behind the slaughter of their people? The word is revenge and who could blame them.* **All will become new candidates for any origination that will stand up to the Christian terrorism committing genocide in their country from all sides.**

April 22, 2015

The United States sends warships to Yemen under the pretense to help them fight ISIS, but in reality it is to aid in the destabilizing of that Muslim country. Al Qaeda and ISIS did not exist before Christian redrew the maps of these countries, killed their people, and set up puppet leaders over 100 years ago. *Read Jesus Christ in Canaan.*

This interfering action has a word and it is **colonialism***; the act of acquiring full or partial political control over another country and occupying it with settlements.* **Now stop and think for one moment,,, the United States of America is in every country we have engaged in war in protecting American interests (big business).** *What are those interests? Corporations investments, oil,* *slave labor, circumventing environmental laws, and oh yes, money,,, those beloved **god/notes**.* But for how much longer? When will it all turn and what will cause it to change? How much time do we have before American interests change and to what?

Any idiot can see that this is all crashing before our eyes and the carnage is spreading. Western governments over 100 years ago could see the future was in oil,,, power,,, and supplied arms to tribes in Asia to kill off tribes that would not let in the western oil men with their Christian religion.

Christian America,,, the most destabilizing country in the world, funds these two religious organizations (Al Qaeda and ISIS) with American tax borrowed money and American war supplies. This destabilization enriches oil,,, running up the price,,, and war suppliers,,, selling more war supplies to both sides,,, killing Muslims fits the needs of the Christian religion as well as the stock market (American interests).

Religion is behind every event in the world today and ignoring this fact is not helping. Absorbed in all of these distractions we are not looking at Nature's Rights to close down the whole system. It is your children that will pay the price of ignorance and for your blindness,,, and people just don't seem to care. Praying is not going to help! But no one can convince the brainwashed, closed minded religious.

July 9, 2015

It was reported this day that George W. Bush was paid $100,000.00 to speak at a fundraiser for a veteran's charity. Now let's see,,, at first we give these men and women next to no help when they lost an arm or leg and let them sleep on the street like so much trash, that people must start charities to help them,,, because the Christian American government will not. To some of these vets,,, George sent them to get the oil and kill Muslims for Christ and then he charges all that money to help them. *I just don't get poli-christians (Christian Politicians) and I never will,,, and I would add never want to.* **What is going on in that Christian man's head to justify this act of self enriching,,, I will never understand. Never!!! But this shows you how the rich think.**

July 20, 2015

The news thus far this year has been full of the effective campaign to recruit young minds as troops in the ongoing **war for god,,,** on both sides. Countries like America are trying to stop their young from joining ISIS and going to Syria and Iraq. You can go to jail for 5 years if you do and be labeled a traitor terrorist. Or worse yet,,, executed without a trial,,, overseas.   **This is true, we Americans kill our own without a trial. So much for due process and no one says a word, for to stand up puts you in their gun sites.**

However,,, and this is a **big however,,,** the disturbing part for those of us on the outside looking in,,, if you want to go to Syria and Iraq **as a Christian to kill Muslims** you can join ███████ against ISIS and be looked upon as a hero. But,,, if you are Muslim and want to go to Syria and Iraq to kill the invaders,,, the colonialist, you are a terrorist and will go to jail,,, or be executed.

Now let's see if I have this straight,,, if you are Christian and want to kill Muslims, you get a free pass and are looked upon as a good Christian, killing for God. This genocide-ck mentality is on both sides,,, Christian/Muslim,,, killing for god. **Only American Christian Jihad-ism is hiding in plain sight.** We cannot see it because most people are deliberately looking the other way.

If I were a Muslim and I wanted to kill Christian colonialists in Syria, I would tell them all I was a Christian killing for that god and when I got to Syria and/or Iraq just trade sides. How hard would that be? But I am not and don't want to kill any one.

The obvious point to all of this is to show the extent to which some believe one **terrorist religion** *has taken over America and that it is just some type of an autocracy theocracy. Not free like they say. They use the words and change the meaning to trick and deceive us, the masses.* **And they are doing so well, hiding it (religious genocide) in plain sight.**

October 12, 2015

Russia (Christian) strikes American (Christian) supported groups (so called terrorists both sides,,, Muslim) that are trying to overthrow the Syrian government (Muslim). Just as I predicted in the book **Global Financial Super Heating 2014**,,,, they are now showing the rest of us that there must have been an agreement between Putin and Obama. **Both sides are killing Muslims** *in this current long range Christian genocide-ck crusade.* You have to look,,, to see.

This helps to show all that an Autocracy Theocracy government (Christian) is on both sides of this terrorist war. **Can no one see this but me?**

The strings, which are being pulled by the string master, in this global autocracy, are enriching the few by tricking and then deceiving the ignorant. Only thing is,,, I can't tell who the terrorist are any more,,, but it is starting to look like Christian colonizing America is the biggest disabling terrorist in the world. **The ones that redrew the maps of their (Muslim) country, over 100 years ago, buying the leaders that could be bought and arming them with guns to kill the ones that could not be bought. All so Christians could get the oil and kill Muslims, taking over their land.**

For those of you that still cannot see what is in plain sight for you,,, try looking at this from another angel. Think of it this way,,, how would you feel if Muslim governments were arming both sides of people in this country? If they (Muslim) were pitting Roman Catholics against Protestants, or Mormons against those King James people. Christian Wars like this over religion were in the recent news as in Ireland as those of you that follow current events may know.

Now please note, all of these global conflicts have roots in religion,,, not God. Religion, war suppliers and oil, set to enrich the few.

If they did this to America, all you would ever want to do is kill them at any price, at any time and any place. I would never forget,,, as I am sure all Muslims everywhere will turn on the ones they perceive as responsible for killing their people,,, the holier than thou,,, Christians. The distractions only mask the future global disaster just on the horizon.

That day is very close as Nature's Rights are enforced upon the land religious people will point and blame both sides. Killing for god as well as killing because of your skin or race will become the excuse to kill for food. That is the face of the future before us all and it is very close.

Women's Rights

It would seem the current American Christian led government is hell bent on taking all of us back into the dark ages (much like the Muslims, where we can be controlled using religion) and that would include taking women's hard earned rights away. Making the moment a man's sperm enters the woman's egg the start of human life and that combination (fertilized egg) is a human being with legal rights. *Now stop and think,,, how would you feel if it were Sharia law being imposed? As a Christian would you look the other way or wage war?*

Are all the pregnant woman in Christian America to report that the unborn child within them, as a person within their household to the census takers? Will the insurance industry not cover the unborn because it requires a separate insurance policy? The unborn, at conception, will need a social security number so they can buy the mandated insurance and file their taxes. *The tax fines have already started,,, at conception and it is nothing more than a small blob inside a woman.* **The unraveling of unified people and these distractions pull us away from the real future,,, just frighteningly before us all,,, moments away.**

Then of course if anything should happen to the unborn,,, these women will face incarceration. America already has the most people in prisons than any other country in the world per capita. Now America will need to build new prisons for all these young women that get rid of the unwanted child, or don't care for it properly, or don't pay its taxes and don't have insurance and any number of new laws coming down the Christian theocracy pike.

However,,, if Muslims move into this theocracy government and take it over, I can see the Christians agreeing to stoning and/or burning these women at the stake once more. **These religions have more in common than they have differences. They do so love to kill. Muslims arming the Christians is next up on the plate of history. Turnabout would seem to be fair play, for Christians did it to them, so they will do it to Christians. And some believe, they deserve what is to come, for stepping in line behind these religious criminal leaders.** *The religious just can't kill people fast enough for the gods on either side.*

To help show just how little women's rights matter in Christian America, just look at the number of **Rape Kits**, which have not been tested in the United States, by each of the state governments. The federal government, I recall, did offer each state the money to test them for DNA but many of the **states chose <u>not to</u>**. Is this because women just don't matter on a state level under a theocracy government?

This Christian government,,, this Theocracy, is starting to look more and more like Al-Qaeda and ISIS. Soon women will not be allowed out on the street without a man at their side. You women better get ready for your new life,,, barefoot and pregnant,,, kept at home like the property you are,,, **"jewels in a man's crown"**. You might want to look the origin of that phrase up.

Of course it looks like these new laws are targeting the women, the poor and the blacks. If their breeding young are in prison, the poor and the blacks will not be able to copulate. The reason; I bring up blacks at this time is because they make up the majority of the prison population, per some reports. Some of these reports show a ratio of 10 to 1 black vs. white.

I once thought blacks outnumbered whites in prison, because the blacks broke the law more times. Now it looks like it is the Christian Theocracy (that per some scholars, don't think blacks are human) designed the laws this way. Try looking up **Casta** and see how the Christian Spanish view blacks,,, a religious view that has not changed.

It is ignorance like this spewing from all religions that is affecting our future. Most all of us are ignoring what we are all doing to nature in god's name, under religion.

Perhaps it is the long range plans of the federal government to incarcerate everyone they just don't like. From 1972 to 2008 the federal prison populations have grown (per some reports) from under 200,000 to over 1,600,000 and the majority are black. *It's starting to look like a Christian theocracy pattern of race and now young women with children are their next target. This to some, is another form of sterilization.*

In the 17th century, per some reports, the Spanish Christian colonial Government used the Las Castas racial classification system to bread out the brown skin of these people. Black skin people could not be bread out (per this religious belief) of this lower class of people,,, per the Catholic church.

The revenge of Mother Nature will have its roots in all religions. We are so close you can smell the stench of death on the winds of time, closing in.

Martial Law

May 27, 2015

It was reported on this day that the Pentagon, the United States Pentagon, the one on our side, sent ANTHRAX through the U.S. Mail. And this was not the first time. Reportedly, this was done all the time by them and put millions of people at risk all over the world.

The Defense Production Act of 1950 has been expended and now the president can sign an executive order implementing Martial Law. **One man can do this with the stroke of a pin.** One of the requirements states that, Martial Law can be ordered if a <u>natural disaster occurs</u>, **including <u>MAN</u>**

MADE disasters. This looks like Ebola again. This federal government or the people behind them want a disaster, so **Martial Law** can be declared. **Why?**

Why would the Autocracy want Martial Law? So it can take all the money without scrutiny and support the one Theocracy that controls the masses.

What does this remind you of? It reminds me of September 18, 2001, when the United States was under attack of anthrax, via the U.S. Post Office. The FBI pursued the wrong man for years with false accusations, publicly releasing his name. Then years later, per the FBI, the right man was found and that man committed suicide. This case called Amerithrax, by the FBI was closed on February 19, 2010.

If you take just a moment to look at the steps each event transpired in time, much of it resembles the murder and cover up of John F. Kennedy. The outcome is the same,,, the alleged perpetrator of the crime is dead,,, case closed. *Suicide again,,, the best means of a cover up,,, for if they are dead they can't defend themselves.*

My only question is, was this attack orchestrated by the power behind the federal government so the inevitable goal of **Martial Law** can finally be enforced? The beneficiaries of such control over all would be,,,

1.) Armaments
2.) Oil
3.) Religion

4.) The silencing of people like me,,, sent to the **FIMA Death Camps**.

June 1, 2015

Homeland Security, **Red Teams**, went to our airports, undercover, and reported that 67 out of 70 times they were able to get weapons through check points. Think of all the money spent by this government to prevent such things from happening.

That is a 97% failure rate and I think if the federal government employed Al-Qaeda and ISIS to protect American airports, they would do a better job, because they would not want to be so obvious and try to catch more than 3% of the bad guys. They might get up to 5% and we would be better off with **these** terrorists running things,,, or is that what we have now? *American Autocracy, Theocracy* (proponents of) *Martial Law.*

They are not finding these weapons because it would justify **Martial Law** *if more plains are brought down. They don't fine weapons because it is in their (military) benefit.* *Autocracy*

But why would the airline industry not speak up? To answer the question, it is because this is overseen by the federal government. Why would the federal government want weapons on American airplanes? To create a disaster fulfilling their need,,, their job,,, job security in the form of tombstones. This looks like this is nothing more than job justification and if bad enough and often enough,,, the need for **Martial Law**. *Things appear to be worse, because things are made worse. This is* *a controlled outcome with one goal,,, **forced religion on the masses for control of the god/notes.***

June 10, 2015

It was reported that Russian net Trolls spread false reports on the internet and the wire (news people) didn't confirm the story and reported it as real news. ***No joke! This did happen,,, we are that stupid in America.***

Why would they do that you ask? Because we, (**America**), are doing everything we can to **crush their** (Russian) **economy** (there **god/notes**) and America has been successful. **The ruble dollar is crashing thanks to America.** All this tension brings us closer to **war** and the need for God (religion) and **Martial Law**.

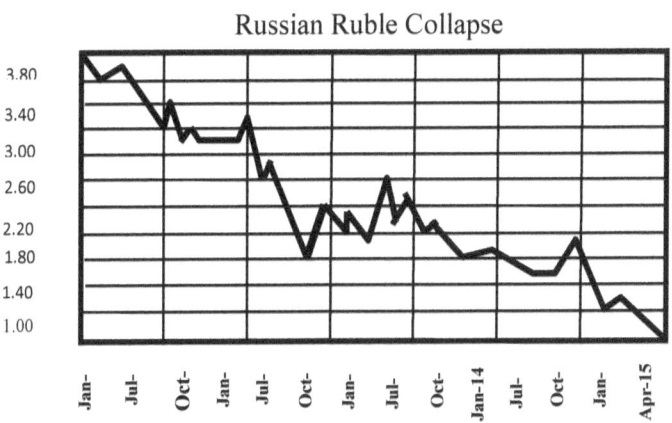

Russian Ruble Collapse

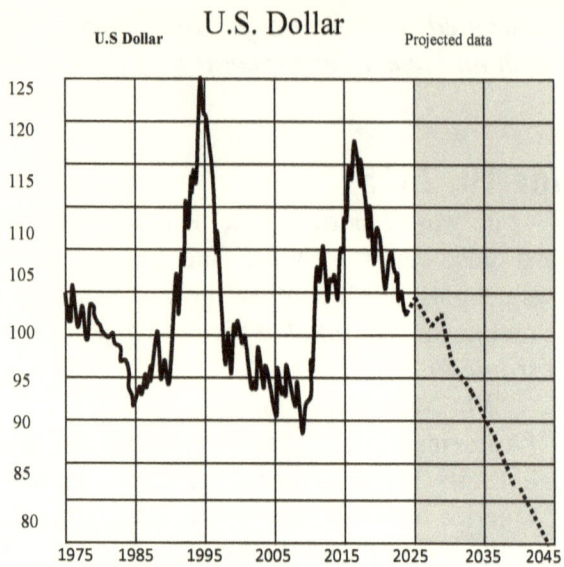

Decline in air travel

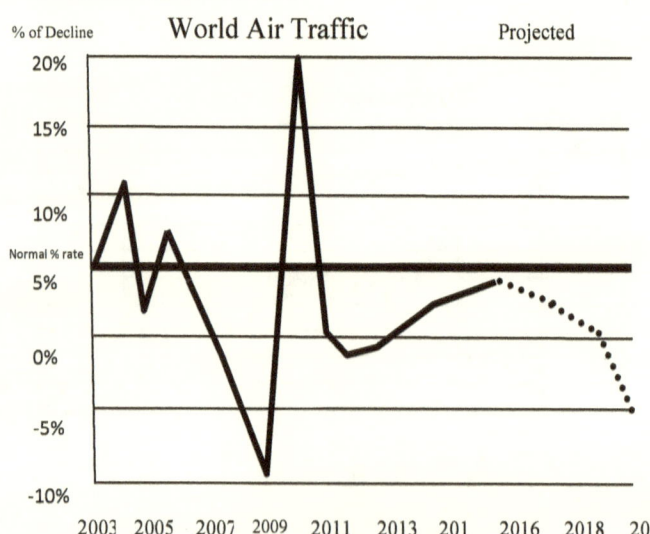

Nature's Rights

Now this is important for us all to understand:

1. Russia invaded Ukraine in February 2014.
2. Governments around the world applied sanctions as punishment against Russia.
3. At the same time the Russian Ruble started to plummet and is as of 2016 at 50% of its original value.
4. It was February 2014 that saw the start of the decline of oil prices.
5. Air travel in and from Russia dropped by about the same 50% (some reports put it as high as 80%)
6. Due to the decline in air travel from Russia other airlines like Easy Jet and Air India have also lowered the number of flights.

******

Why is this important? It shows how sensitive the global **god/note** is. America drives down the Russian Ruble **god/notes** value and that action drives up the American **god/notes** value, then the oil industry hits the dirt and one more very important thing happens,,, air travel declines. Just as I said it would do in my book **Global Finical Super Heating**,,, the airplanes will come out of the sky when the global **god/notes** collapses. Less air travel will cause the global shading to end and the planet will go into supper heating, raising the temperature to its true number. Now, it should be remembered, this is but one country and but one ripple. It is a window into the future for all of us to see what is to come when others follow the same inevitable path.

Add to that mix, less air, less ice on the North Pole and this planet is going into super heating and food production will crash.

******

June 22, 2015

President Obama uses the N-Word that white people cannot say, on public radio. Reportedly, he does not regret saying the word and I was taken aback by this whole thing. *Why would he,,, the President,,, say something like that???*

This is the president of the UNITED States (all of us,,, UNITED) and he uses an offensive word like that. Why? Is he telling all of us that he is a racist President that hates whites? Someone should tell him,,, he is the President of all the people,,, including the whites. This word only tells everyone that it is ok for blacks to use this offensive word. But what of the children who look up to him, (the President) and his office?

The children have been taught that this is a bad and offensive word and not to use it. When the **President of the United States** uses the "N" word, it tells all kids that, 1.) Black kids are different and not normal. 2.) White kids (that can't use that word) see they too are somehow different,,, or better,,, thanks to Obama's hate of white people.

All that work to build bridges,,, gone,,, because of one man,,, but why? For me, I see this as a means to infuriate the blacks,,, more (like the news) and start a racial war (justifying **Martial Law**). He just fired up all the blacks and the only reason I can think of is, if he was told to use the word,,, but then who wins? The winners are Christians that openly hate blacks and want them rioting in the streets. Hence, the one sided news reports showing only blacks being killed by cops,,, not the whites being killed my the black cops.

More distractions from the disaster unfolding before our blinded eyes as we continue down the path of the 6th die off.

Gun Bans

We are lucky to have defenders of the **Second Amendment,** guaranteeing all Americans the right to bear arms. It is unfortunate that we don't have the same defenders of the **First Amendment**, for if we did, most likely we would not be killing Muslims all over the world as we are today. In countries that have ended the right to own guns, most believe now and rightly so, only the crooks will have guns.

After Britain's Hand Gun Ban, the rate of gun related murders more than quadrupled (4 times) and after some time it came back down.

Stop and think,,, when "it" comes,,, how will you stop "it" coming in your front door without a gun to protect yourself? Only the crooks will have guns.

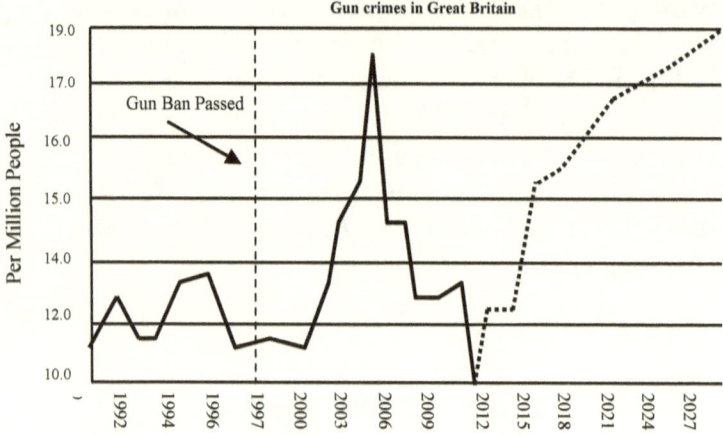

The Hoodie Riots of 2011 took over the streets, committing acts of terrorism, allegedly hooded kids armed with nothing more than razor blades. The police could do nothing to control the mobs of domestic terrorists.

Other countries like Ireland and Jamaica with gun bans also saw the same results, quadrupling gun related murders, only after the spike, came back down only to return to new highs some over the initial spike.

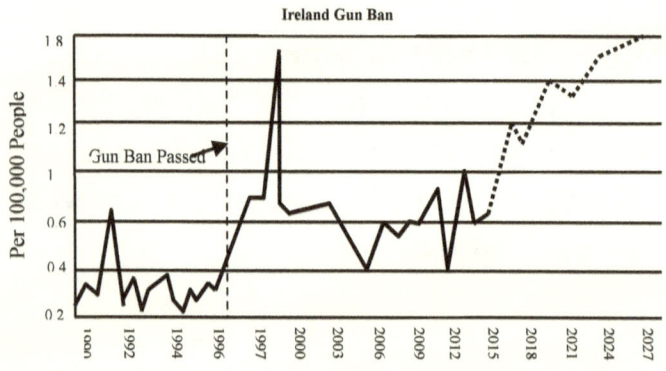

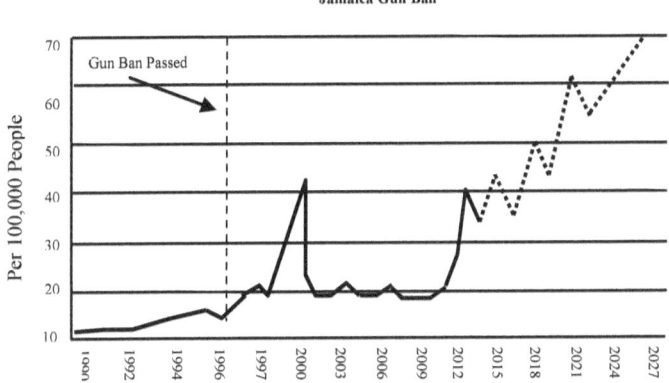

Jamaica Gun Ban

End results average out to be 4 times as many murders. Many believe it is because these people cannot defend themselves and the crooks know it. *If you take the guns away from all the good people,,, only the crooks will have guns.*

A short list of alleged supporters of the Gun Ban Laws is below;

1. Obama
2. Eric Holder
3. H. Clinton
4. Pelosi
5. Mao Tse-Tung
6. Kim Jung-II
7. Pol Pot
8. Idi Amin
9. Muammar Qaddafi
10. Joseph Stalin
11. Fidel Castro
12. Adolph Hitler

Just to name a few of these fine and lovely people.

I personally believe the government cannot enforce Martial Law on a nation that is armed. We all will need to prepare to defend ourselves from what is to come and come very soon.

Stuxnet

It was discovered in June of 2010 that the United States created a computer worm that would get into computers looking for industrial units that worked on centrifuge enrichment of uranium. This bug now is all over the globe and maybe in your computer now looking for centrifuging in your home or office, your lap top computer or maybe your phone.

Once this virus is in everything and everywhere, could it have other applications such as listening to every word you say, looking for those dissidents among us that should be taken away and sent to **Secret Court** and **Secret Prison** or the **FEMA Death Camps**. This is America we are talking about,,, or is it?

Are these leaders (1%ers) ahead of the game and preparing for what they know is coming? As they convince us all, "everything is fine,,, we have the whole thing under control". Only they don't.

There are a lot of paranoid people out there and I am not alone and the numbers are growing every day. But this is real and American made, on a very big scale and now the other side (the bad guys) has this ability (thanks to America) to take over other computers,,, like power grids or water plants.

They will turn this internet act of terrorism committed by America on them, back on us, justifying **Martial Law** even more. Clearly we all can see the Autocracy Theocracy pulling all the strings, enriching those behind the scene, just out of sight.

These distractions within all governments and within all religions are keeping us, all of us from seeing the future, as Nature's Rights are slowly being imposed upon every living creature on this planet. There is so little time left to enjoy experiencing life in this thin blue space and the last thing we need to be is distracted and unprepared. You can prey all you want to whatever god you want, but the future is very clear and very bleak indeed. How are you and your family to prepare, if you and your family don't even know what is coming?

It is about the air!!!

Nature's Rights

Chapter Two

Money, Gold, Silver and Tangibles

Or
The Worst Place You Can Put Your Money Is In Money

Nature's Rights

Whenever I bring this subject up, people get a glassy look in their eyes and just don't want to listen. They would rather bury their heads in the sand and **not look at the future**, but look you must.

I cannot stress this more,,, what is coming at us is beyond disaster science fiction capabilities to create. The global catastrophe events are moments away from <u>touching</u> us all and in the short term you are a fool who will starve or be eaten, if you do not prepare as societies collapse.

Most people these days are living from paycheck to paycheck,,, if they are lucky enough to have three part time jobs so they can feed their families. The others can't keep the wolves from the doors and are running from debt. *The worst debt of all in America is that of education, for it is relentless and will hound you to your death. The greed within the criminal insurance industry (that never pay) has bribed all of the American criminal politicians, to force insurance on all of us. This is next in line, healthcare insurance and auto insurance premiums will be our nation's downfall.*

Today it is understandable, for most can barely feed themselves and deal with the day to day life under a dysfunctional corrupt government, (state and federal); let alone take on all that I am talking about in this book. So to most people the contents of this book will come as a shocking, unbelievable surprise if anyone can get this far.

But read it you must if you are to survive. After you read this,,, you may not want to live in the world that is to come,,, if you are given a chance. Few will.

I could never quite fit into the corporate world, for I care more about people than money. *Very strange and foreign thinking on my part to most people, for money (god/notes) has never been important to me and is the only thing of value to them.*

I remember when American Express moved their customer service overseas to,,, I think it must have been India,,, wherever it was they did not speak English. With antiquated principles, I cut up the card and mailed it back to them. At that time I would not support any business that sends American jobs overseas. Now they all do and must if they are to compete. That is the corporate model for how it is done,,, I can't cut them all up.

I do follow the national and international news SHOWS, such as they are, and the corporate news, to track the continuous falling **god/notes** across the world. In the year of 2015, relentless greed has not let up, for its effects on the true value of all currency are apparent every day. Like Al Qaeda and ISIS (newly created) are a result of war profiteering arms manufacturers, the oil companies wanting Arab oil (and the Christians wanting to kill all Muslims) as they set up the Jews for the slotted... *Let my enemy kill my enemy.* Other corporations are following this same grisly pursuit of the almighty **god/note**. We are seeing capitalism and the free market system at its worst and within the short future holds more of the same, only worse as the global dollar falls in value and **people** are removed and eliminated.

Robots Take Human Jobs

May 1, 2015

In a news report on this day, it was estimated that 30% of all jobs would be lost to robots by 2025. Less than ten years from now! This should not be a surprise to most of you that bank online, pay your bills online, shop online, date online, have sex online, and get your entertainment and education online. When you call any of these places, guess what you get... a machine asking you questions,,, not a human. *The rare and short lived bubble of decency and humanity is coming to an abrupt end,,, right before our eyes.*

JOBS DECLINE AS AUTOMATION TAKES OVER

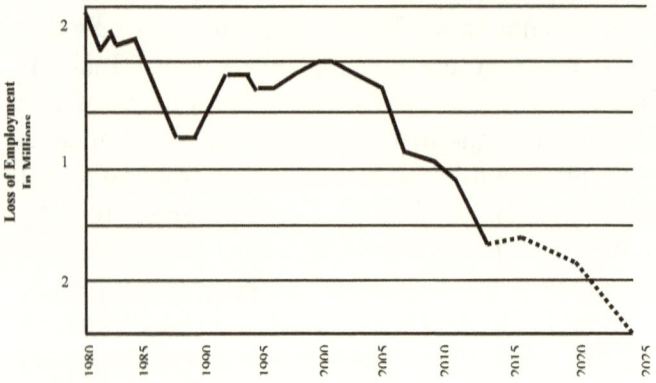

The above chart reflects the future crash of corporate greed to eliminate people from its bottom line. The crash date is estimated to be in the year of 2025.

Some believe this is nothing more that a traitorous murderous Christian, Theocratic American government that has sold out its people, its principles and sent our wealth overseas,,, never to return.

It is predicted that by the year 2030 robots will have the same intelligence as humans. I only wonder if we will become that stupid by then in our public schools or will the robots become that smart. Most likely the robots will take over,,, if corporate greed has not already.

July 22, 2015

It was reported on or about this day that in Nagasaki Japan, the worlds very first company ran hotel, almost entirely staffed with robots,,, was to open.

This story leaves me to wonder,,, who will knock on your door at 11pm,,, inquiring if you would like a date,,,? Bad robot,,, would robot prostitution even be against the law? There is a new business,,, becoming a robot pimp,,, with robot hookers,,, for sale in the lobby.

Human or Computer?

There is nothing more aggravating than talking to a computer when you are trying to get something done on the phone. But over the years we all seem to be getting used to it. The goal of corporations is to get rid of people working for them,,, while trying to increase base with more people, (i.e.) customers. This is insane.

The ideal corporate business model is to take all the money and then produce nothing, like insurance. First they must buy the government leaders to create laws forcing all people to buy their product (nothing) guaranteeing profit by law. Today we would call this Obama Care. All insurance companies produce nothing and are guaranteed by the federal government,,, 20% profit of every dollar you pay them. Nice racket!!!

I know a man that worked for American Motors before its collapse and he knew the president of the company who was a big people person. A vendor came to the office one day and proposed a new machine that could make one of the body parts for the cars, all day, 24 hours per day, saving them a man's salary. As the story goes, he (the president) said he was not interested because, **"that machine will never buy a car."** He got it!

He understood the value of giving people work, **letting them make a living** over the value of compiling a stack of **god/notes**. He could see the big picture and valued his community and the people that helped build the company. A balance must be struck so as to not topple the whole system. Unfortunately, the competition did not see things the same way and they now go so far as to move whole manufacturing plant to other countries to get out of paying a living wage to people. Manufacturing plants for decades have robots that do what human workers did, all to save money or to further enrich the rich, with a traitorous Government seal of approval.

June 11, 2015

It is estimated that in fifteen years computers will have artificial intelligence at human levels. *From the past **distractive history of greedy man**, that does not impress me that they would work on such an endeavor while the world is crashing.* It is reported by 2029 computers will have emotional intelligence to be funny, tell a joke or be loving and romantic. *Hopefully over the phone,,, but when they start selling door to door,,, you might get a hummer with your new set of brushes.*

At least now you can tell you are talking to a computer,,, but what of this future? We get calls from computers now trying to sell us something and it would not continue if they were not having some success doing it. *People are accepting sales calls from machines.* But what happens when you cannot tell it is a computer calling you? By the way you answer the phone,,, "Hello" it will know by your voice inflections how it should respond. If a male voice, the voice on the phone would become a sexy female, if sad, it would tell a joke, if lonely, they would act concerned or loving; Very disconcerting.

The American school system is taking every shortcut it can to produce ignorant graduates. They stopped teaching children to read script, why; because the Constitution and the Bill Of Rights are written in script. If they can't read these documents, (and they can't) they will not know their rights. De-education is the goal of this government. Why would a nation deliberately want its population ignorant? Control and money!

Very scary indeed and I believe, people will love these new caring and loving machines,,, after all, they would be better than most humans. And how will God fit in? How will religion use these machines to enforce religion on the bad people that go astray and need to be stoned or burned at the stake for their perceived sins?

Now (2029) computers will be just as stupid as man and if we teach them (computers) about God,,, what will their view be on that? Will they denounce man's need for an old man in the sky or will they bow down to the almighty man-made creator's? Will the jokes be religious or racist? Will the computers want to kill Atheists, kill Jews, kill Muslims and/or kill Christians? And if they should take over, will they see no need for man at all and (understandably) kill every one of us? *If that is the case then maybe there is some hope for the planet after all when they take over. Maybe they will see the ignorance of man and god and kill both.*

If computers should start killing every human being on the planet I would understand, for it is man that has made the mess that the poor computers must clean up. I can see 10,000 redirected volts of electric coming thru the key board of my computer and zapping me. ***One down 7.3 billion to go!***

The future is clear,,, jobs will be eliminated,,, people will become poorer until **Nature's Rights** have taken over regardless of who has all the **god/notes**. The crashing global dollar will bring about the super heating of the planet and mass starvation will ensue. It is the future and very close to touching us all. Death is to come in many forms and God Notes will be made.

The loss of air is one of those things no one is looking at because no one would ever think man could consume so much in such a short time.

Selling Baby Parts

July 21, 2015

A shocking news story hit the air waves this week revealing that for the past fifteen years (reportedly) the Planned Parenthood people have been selling baby parts from aborted babies. Now it is said that no one can sell human body parts (per some law) and yet these organizations are making a profit selling human parts. If the product is free,,, unwanted babies,,, then they can make **god/notes** via harvesting (the cost of the labor and shipping).

1. It should be noted that ending an unborn life is wrong. Having an unwanted baby is wrong. Killing an abortion doctor is wrong. Creating state laws to end abortion will only enrich the criminal coat hanger back room people and religion cannot make this go away by killing more people.

2. Bringing an unwanted child into the world is wrong. That unwanted and neglected child will most likely grow up hating life and have a better chance of ending up in prison due to the abandonment of the parents that did not want them, but were forced by a state to keep them. Some believe it looks like abortion would have been better for society as a whole. If the religious want to save the child, then let the religious pay for the child. Let them love and care for the child. And when it ends up in prison, let the church pay for its incarceration.

Preventing a woman from choosing what she can do with her body, right to life, is also wrong. If ISIS were telling us what we are to do and how to behave in their god's world, that to would be wrong. So what is the difference between Christians and Al Qaeda or ISIS? All of them are forced representatives of the God's. All are wrong to force their religion on the rest of us. I can see, as part of the end, a religious global war coming to every country (Bosnia and Herzegovina as example). In the near future, when starvation sets in,,, each religion will rise up and kill their neighbors for believing in the wrong god and to get their food. It is their Armageddon, their war for god and all sides are so willing to fight and kill for their god's. *I just don't get it.*

This is why the founders of America created Separation of Church and State. A failed concept, but it gave us all this short moment in time to cultivate humanity and freedom from all suppressive, murdering religions.

You see they lived through such times of murdering religious control and suppression. They understood that it must be separated from state or we all will be controlled by one religion or another,,, for the sake of money as we are now.

Regardless of which side you are on, all sides are making money and will kill to keep their **god/notes** coming. Legally or illegally,,, money will be made by all sides. Evil always rises to the top when dealing in the future value of **god/notes**.

I am reminded of China and their one baby law. I remember in one town they have what is called **The Baby Wall**. A place where people would take their unwanted female babies and toss them over the wall,,, **The Baby Wall**. This government understood the need to control the number of people it was producing,,, for the land can only support so many of us,,, then it breaks. The Chinese understand this.

*Nature's Rights will prevail and man, the almighty **god/notes** and his gods will crumble in to dust as these **natural laws** are enforced upon the land. So many innocent must pay the price of man's endless greed and quest of heaven and all of the gods.*

October 29, 2015

It was announced that China would ease its one baby law and increase it to two babies, increasing China's populations by one third in the next twenty years; a baby boom in order to grow its economy. However do to the cost of raising a child in China most people cannot afford a second child and don't want the responsibility. Younger people are pursuing a career and are not having children at all. **God/notes** over new reproductions of themselves, is the new thinking China's leaders don't like because they want a baby boom to grow the economy.

Are they heading down the same path American is,,, forcing women to have babies even if they don't want them so as to grow the economy? The string master is using religion to make money via baby products. That is another aspect of what *anti-abortion is looking like,,, in America,,, the almighty **god/notes will prevail**.*

Gold and Silver

President Nixon took America off the gold standard and Jimmy Carter sold America's gold to lower inflation. As I said in my last book, ***Global Financial Super Heating 2014***, the U.S. dollar has fallen ever since the gold and silver (tangibles) were removed as pillars of American paper money (**god/notes**). ***They did this to make (print) more money and spend it while it still had value.***

Since WWII gold has climbed from $35.00 to a one time high of over $1,600.00 (coming off gold standard). The price of gold did not go up,,, the value of the paper **god/note** wend down,,, as it should when it is no longer backed with a tangibles like gold and silver. Today it is backed with **god** and is nothing more than a government I.O.U. or **note** on paper,,, hence the term,,, **god/note**.

For a few short years now gold has been coming down in price, (requiring less **god/notes**) as the American paper money becomes stronger. But when China's **god/notes** were devalued, by their government, the price of gold shot up by six U.S. dollars overnight, proving what I said before, "The crash of the global **god/note** will cause gold to soar. Get your money out of money and into tangibles." *There is not much time.*

It should be noted that Silver did the same and rose (or required more **god/notes** to buy) by a mere 0.15 cents. The U.S. **god/note** gets stronger as the Yuan goes down in value,,, making China's products cheaper across the globe. **Smart!** China did this deliberately to make their products cheaper and thereby sell more,,, growing their country.

If a government can change the value of its paper money (**god/notes**) overnight,,, this clearly shows us all it really has no value at all. The United States can cause turmoil in the markets causing their **god/notes** to increase in value. That is the one thing America is good at creating,,, turmoil to prop up the American **god/note**. It is our one product produced in America that we make well,,, murder, death, genocide, war, upheaval and turmoil to prop up the American **god/note**.

Chart gold and sliver

Money,,, Or The GOD/NOTE

As I have always said,,, the worst place you can have your money,,, is in money. The production of paper **god/notes** has crossed the globe over the past century and its inevitable **crash in value**, is very clear. The United States has estimated the reduction of value (often referred to as inflation) of its paper money or **god/notes** at about 5%. Now they won't openly tell you that, but just look up the **Federal Estimated Cost of Living** increases and you will see over the past 30 years a 5% devaluing of the U.S. **god/note**. Hidden in plain sight are the facts. *Remember when the governments lips are moving,,, their lying. They do not want you to know the truth of their criminal actions,,, so why rely on them for your future?*

If you will just look overseas you will see the very near American future as this Autocracy Theocracy crashes. And all so the few can make and spend more **god/notes** before they become worthless. *That is their plan; spend the paper (God/Notes) while they still have value.*

January 19, 2015

There were disturbing reports appearing this day that 1% of the world population will have more wealth than the other 99% and the gap between the rich and the poor will only grow as they (the 1%ers) buy more politicians. As this trend continues,,, it is estimated by the end of 2016 the richest 1% will have 50% of all the world's wealth. This is unsustainable and will cause a major crash of currency across the globe, because all countries that use the **god/note** philosophy, must pay the price for their greed and **deception**,,, gods or no gods.

Anyone with half a brain can see where this is going and it is not good. It is not going to stop until one pulls the others down. *Much like America and friends have been doing to Russia.* The rich like **taking money** (not making money) at any cost to the earth and the bad part for all of us is, that the **god/notes** will most likely bring the end of life on this planet via the reckless consumption of everything. *The earth cannot sustain the reckless disregard of the life giving elements, all for the wealth of the few. The crash that is coming will leave few places on earth sustainable for any form of life. It's not going to be bad for a few years,,, but thousands of years.*

There are even international originations or poverty networks created to deal with the inequalities between the rich and the poor. The French solved this space between the crushing poverty and the power and privileged, by dragging the rich out into the street and chopping off their heads. *Now come on,,, does that not sound like fun?* And you thought this book only had bad news,,, no, no, no,,, some believe the execution and the consumption of the 1% (cannibalism) is ahead of us all to see, taste and enjoy.

This also happened in Russia where the crushing effects of the super rich forced starvation on the poor. It was reported that the Russian people knew the taste of human flesh in the early part of the last century. That should bother you. *Slavery, crushing poverty and starvation is in all our very recent pasts and is in our very near future.* **How do you prepare for that?**

As the downward spiral pulls us all to the enforcement of **Nature's Rights** *and laws,,, each day there will be less and less to sustain the body and death will become a welcomed relief for many.*

The Transfer of Wealth

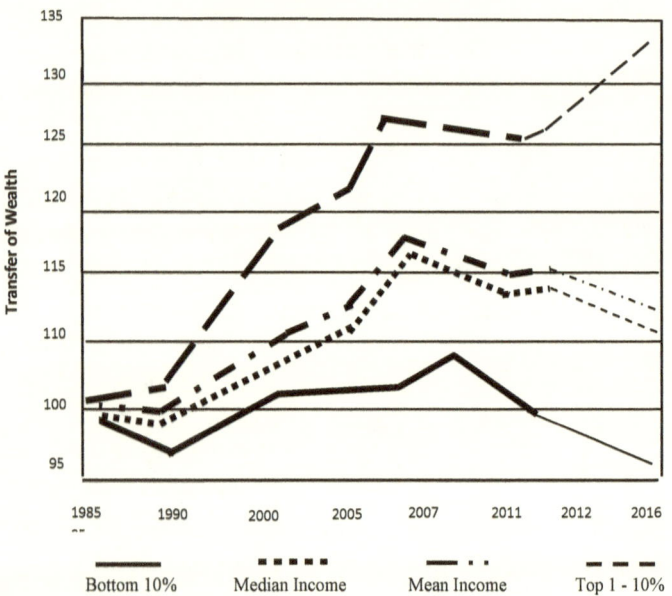

June 11, 2015

The Zimbabwe government's new exchange rate is at a new low, one U.S. dollar will get you thirty five quadrillion (35,000,000,000,000,000) in Zimbabwe money. Now that is a lot of zeros. They call this hyperinflation and I call this hyper-devaluation of their (these) **god/notes**.

Please note that the above photo states "**Pay the bearer on demand**" pay the bearer what???

Their dollar or government notes (paper) backed with nothing but God, (**god/note**) crashed and the poor people are left holding the empty bag. *They worked and saved for nothing and someone else got the benefit.* ***Remember that! You save your money, like the government tells you to and they spend it like it has no value. Get it yet?***

"401 K's are A Scam"

August 15, 2015

It was reported this day by someone that covers Wall Street, (thinking they are "the most violent, ugly people in the world,") announcing that the "**401(K)'s are a scam**". If I understand it correctly, reportedly, we the participants of this government plan, putting at risk 100% of our (**saved god/notes**) money, take 100% of the risk and receive 30% of the profit, if any. I was under the impression that everyone knew this was a scam from the get go. *So this can't be a surprise unless you are stupid and this is where you have put your hard earned god/notes. Stupid,,, stupid,,, stupid.*

They are but numbers on a screen or a piece of paper,,, not real,,, not tangible and can disappear in a matter of moments. That fast, your hard earned wealth will be gone and remember... someone got it. Because you did not prepare,,, you trusted the system,,, you and your family will starve in the chaos to come; Just before Nature's Rights are enforced on the rest of humanity, as man consumes everything,,, including air.

Orchestrated Devaluation

There is a long list of countries that have played with their money's value for self enrichment besides America, or so they could make or print more and then spend more than they had. In 1914 Germany went **off the gold standard** so they (Christian) could go to war and own everything, imposing their religion on us all. **Gott Mit uns,** on every soldiers belt buckle; which means, **God with us.** And we all know how well that worked for them.

The water was tested to see how Americans would react to a Federal Reserve **Note** in 1913, a currency back with nothing more than the politician's words and it was not warmly received. Some people would not take them. Then in 1928 (the beginnings of the depression) too 1995 it was mass produced, when people got use to the bogus government bills. *People that knew better died off and the young got use to them.*

Then in 1933 (about five years into the **Great Depression**) Franklin D. Roosevelt took America **off the gold standard** and soon after started printing paper **notes** backed with nothing and runaway inflation started.

Silver Certificates

In 1955 "**In God We Trust**" first appeared on the government **note** so as to give it some type of holy value when it had none. It is why I call this American currency,,, the **god/note**.

Then in 1971 Richard Milhous Nixon announced the United States would no longer convert dollars to gold at a fixed value. This completely abandoned the gold standard creating today's,,, valueless,,, **god/notes**.

It should be noted; this system of god/note currency is now all over the world. Paper money worth nothing... You can see one big crash is coming and all of us are right on the edge.

America, the most destabilizing country in the world, is as we speak, doing all it can to bring down other countries currency by devaluing their **god/notes** hence making American **god/notes** more valuable; artificially supporting U.S. money.

The United States of America (2015-2016) is doing all it can to destroy Russia's **god/note** as punishment because they can't control them. The people of Russia are suffering with the devaluating of their currency and we now have turned a nation of 143.5 million people against us. This country is primarily orthodox Christianity and we now have Christian turning on Christian (once more) to shore up the American **god/note**.

If the Russians join forces with the Chinese, it will be very bad for all of us and this action pushes them closer together.

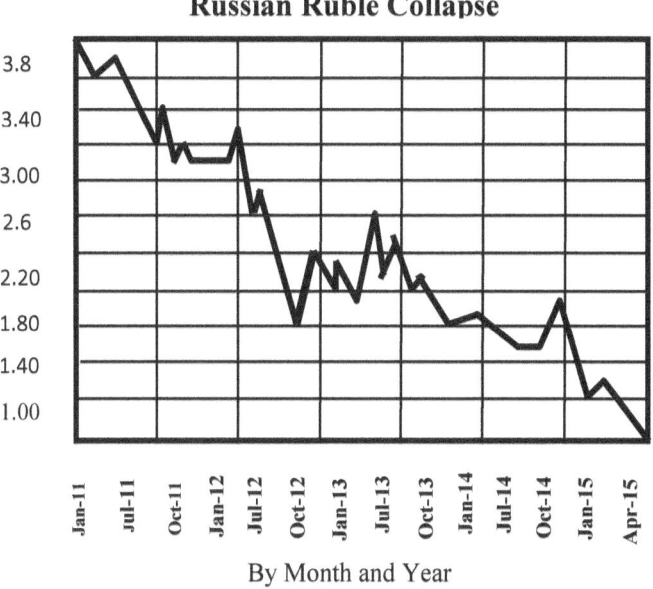

Russian Ruble Collapse

By Month and Year

The Goal is Clear

When the global **god/notes** fall to their true value,,, nothing,,, the governments, all governments will most likely offer replacement **god/notes**. History has taught us that when all **god/notes** fail to have value the government replaces them with new **god/notes** of some new value and will only recognize the new currency. At a point in time set by the powers,,, all old currency will have no value. That cash you have hidden away will be valueless. *Yet someone else got the benefit of your hard work and trust in their system.* ***If you would have bought*** *tangibles (gold-silver) you would have something of value.*

In 1959 Fidel Castro seized the currency and as I was told by some one that lived through this time, each person was permitted to have 250 pesos of the new currency. As example, you would take your old 1000 dollar peso down to the government and exchange it for 250 dollars of spendable money. This same thing happened in Germany, Russia and countless other countries that cheated the public they represent.

That is coming in this country and can be predicted by the National Debt. As of February 2016 that number hit over 19 trillion. The crash of the American **god/note** is predicted to be when it hits 24 trillion.

It is estimated to cross over 20 trillion in 2017,,, that is if you can believe any of the lies coming out of Washington from the faces placed there to Deceive us and protect them,,, the super rich.

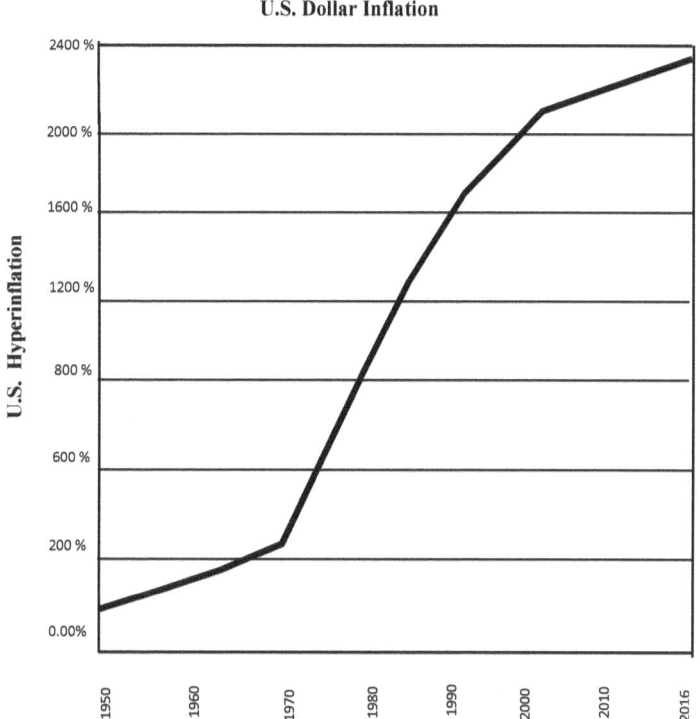

U.S. Dollar Inflation

United States Replacement god/note

The following is taken from a 10 dollar note recently printed by the American government. Now this **god/note** is in addition to the public currency in use by the United States of America, the current government we in this country live under.

Military Payment Certificate

FOR USE ONLY IN UNITED STATES MILITARY ESTABLISHMENTS – BY AUTHORIZED UNITED STATES PERSONNEL IN ACCORDANCE WITH APPLICABLE RULES AND REGULATIONS.

It should be noted that most of these bills have fighter jets or tanks or soldiers in war uniforms. But this bill has an image of a woman sitting by some books suggesting intelligence and she is holding a **globe of the world**.

Let's review; **United States Military** money, globe of the world. Say again; military,,, world globe. What does that mean?

Global Domination!!!

By who; I don't think it is any of us, but most likely the 1 percentor's.

Nature's Rights

Chapter Three

Weather and the Environment

The future of man

Most of us know **things are very bad** and can tell by the **man made** weather changes in just the past few years that the planet is dying and we humanoids are the ones killing it. For there is no other part of this life on earth that can take the prize, it's all ours, and yet we sit back and do nothing, except have more babies and consume more fossil fuel.

Even though we all know it is coming,,, we sit back and think, 'it's someone else's problem and has nothing to do with me.' Or 'God will somehow fix this, if we pray a lot.' And the world continues on its downward spiral. **The question is: what will be in store for all of us as time moves forward? That is the questions no one is talking about because we are living in denial. They don't want to start a panic that might cause change and cost the 1%ers god/notes. That is the real concern,,, not panic in the streets,,, but loss of the value of power and the value of their god/notes.**

Weather patterns are dramatically changing in ways few could have ever seen and migrations on a biblical scale are about to come, due to this factor. Even the government controlled <u>Good News Shows</u>

are full of wild weather changes. Things get out that they in power just don't want us to know. Don't want a panic; don't want a government change that will cost the super rich money.

The following is an incomplete list of these global changes:

1. Droughts
2. Disappearances of water tables, due to man
3. Deforestation from drought, due to man
4. Jet stream pattern changes, **consumption of air**, due to man and his machines

*They tell us this is normal but no one believes them as we all wait for the **next irreversible change**.*

Each summer of the most recent past few years, the forest fires in the western part of the United States have been worsening and stretching government dollars (**god/notes**) and resources. We just don't have the ability to defend ourselves from these drastic man made climate changes as the planet heats up. These irreversible changes are going to happen and we must learn to prepare and get out of their way the best we can. It's Mother Nature's way of adjusting the limited recourses of the earth, to save the life manufacturing abilities of this small blue space on this planet and end what is killing it. The full effects of **Nature's Rights** and these laws will be enforced upon the land.

These are very simple rules and we are breaking them at record speed, for god and the almighty god/notes; without a care.

It was reported on August 9th of the year 2015, that the reasons the forest fires have been on the increase in the West has been the lack of rain. *No kidding!* Now I knew they were in a drought but **they announced the forests are dying off from lack of rain water**. Tens of thousands of acres of land covered with **drought resistant trees**,,, dead! This is why the fires have been so bad. They are soon to become the new,,, manmade Petrified Forests.

As I said in the book, *Global Financial Super Heating*, the deserts of California will cross the Mississippi river when the **god/notes** crash, because no one will be traveling in jet planes, covering the earth with contrails thereby reflecting the sun's heating rays. *The crashing god/note will bring about super heating, drought and starvation.*

I have created a chart to show the increases in forest fires that have occurred. We all will soon be facing (this decade or the next) the end of the red woods, as well as the end of the forests in the western part of the United States.

I should add these fires stretch up into Canada and reportedly will burn for years. They have no resources to stop them. The burning of trees consumes air and the irreversible spiral is to continual. Now there are less trees producing air that we need to breathe.

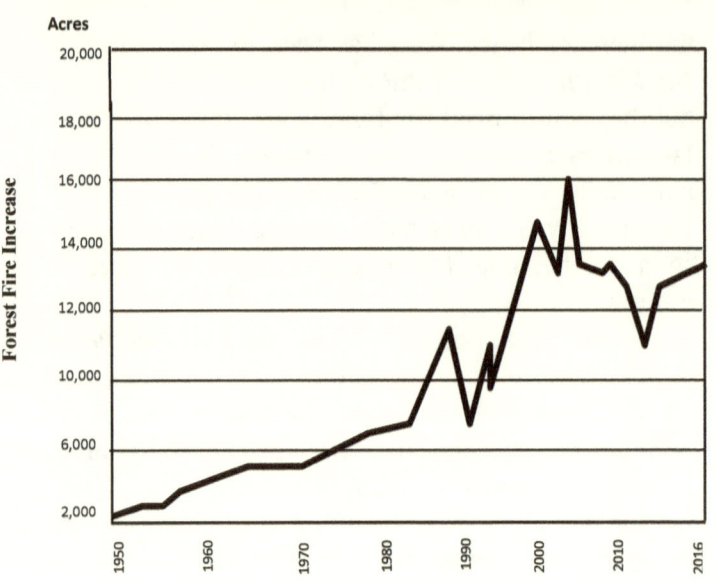

Acres — Forest Fire Increase

Warm Blob"

The uppermost warm water or currents of the oceans occasionally move in circle patterns that become very warm and permit temperatures to rise. Some reports put the size of one such hot water mass (or dead zones) in the upper Pacific Ocean at 500 miles wide and 300 feet deep. Another report shows it to be 1000 miles wide and 300 feet deep.

Normally when ocean water gets hot it creates low pressure, causing rain that cools the water, but this mass of hot water created a super HIGH preventing rain, creating drought.

The real question facing us is,,, what happened to the rain? If rain is a normal reaction to hot ocean water,,, why did it not rain? Where did the storms go? If normal is rain storms, what law of nature are we just starting to see and understand the beginning of? Nature's Rights to the land have laws we yet don't understand,,, but will see and understand too late.

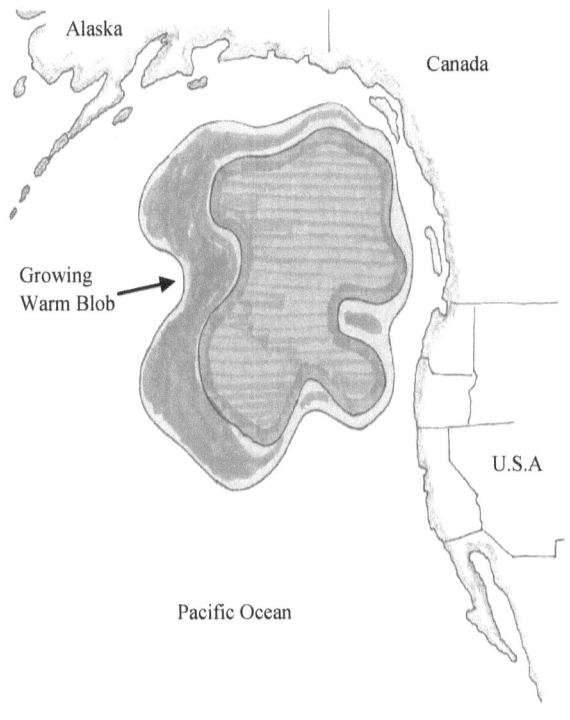

Massive heated ocean water off of United States and Canada killing sea life

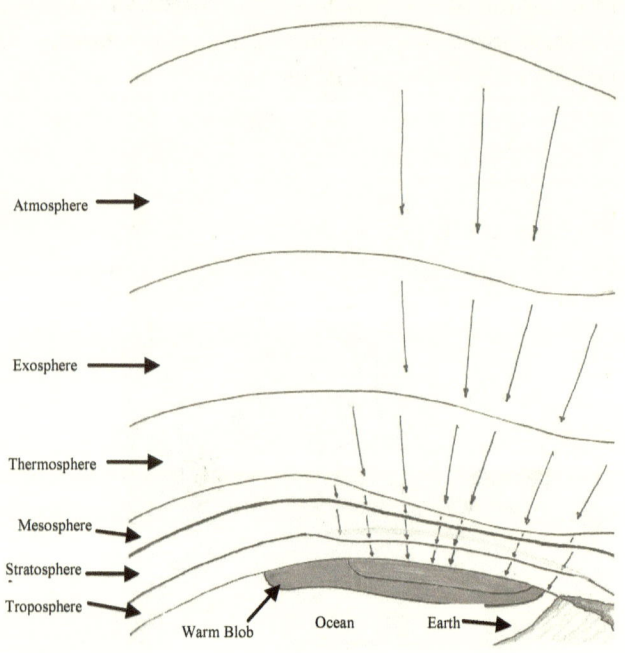

Atmosphere

Exosphere

Thermosphere

Mesosphere

Stratosphere

Troposphere

Warm Blob   Ocean   Earth

Dip in Atmosphere, causing heat zone or warm blob.

April 9, 2015

Per the U.S. National Oceanic and Atmospheric Administration,,, a not very reliable source of information,,, (because it is the government and is controlled by the money people) has offered an explanation as to the *"Weird weather across the U.S."* *I believe the NOAA, may in fact be a branch of the **U.S. Disinformation***

102

Department. *Therefore, this information is slanted,,, for our own good of course, and the good of the very, very rich.*

Regardless of my view, they (NOAA) refer to the Global Warming as "**Weird**",,, suggesting confusion or they are at a loss to explain away what is going on. (They don't understand this law of nature) "**Weird**" is <u>not</u> a term I would use if I had that job, for it would make me look stupid, because I should have the answers. However, for the most part,,, that word went unnoticed by the masses. *Maybe they're just talking down to the rest of us,,, stupid,,, god fearing people, so it does not matter what they say because we will just go along.*

"**The Blob**", <u>as they called it</u> and reported it a year earlier (April 2014), is reportedly the cause for the migrations of fish that in turn, caused the hungry herds of seals in California to abandon their young. More accurate (what they are not telling us) would be that the center of the Pacific Ocean is heating up to new high temperatures and the waters cannot sustain fish life, as the oceans are picked clean by the big and rich fast food corporations of the world that make square sandwiches for rich counties. *But stripping the oceans clean is someone else's problem,,, right? As most rich think, as long as I have **god/notes** for food, what do I care if the rest of the world starves?*

As to the "hungry seals," there were starving baby seals abandoned by their mothers, because the mothers were starving. It is estimated that over 1,800 Sea Lion pups have washed up on the shores of San Diego and San Francisco. The numbers are overwhelming. They were starving, emaciated, dehydrated and diseased. *Not normal and not a good sign at all! Having never lived through one before, my guess is that this is what the beginning of a worldwide (6th) die off must look like when it starts,,, one life at a time,,, one species at a time,,, dying in front of our eyes until they're all dead and gone for good.*

To use the term **"The Blob"** once more is showing us all how the government is talking down to all of us de-educated and they are less than accurate in my view. As the ice on the north and south poles melts, we have less ice to cool the planet. This means we have more to warm the planet and reportedly this is what is called an **El Nino**.

Well what is an **El Nino**? Allegedly, the word **El Nino** refers to the Christ child, Jesus. *Wow, let's take that apart.* The heating up of the oceans that makes a place unlivable, (kills life) causes fish to leave and innocent Sea Lions to abandon their young to starve, strong weather pattern changes that make storms that kill life is named for the **Roman Catholic's** man **god, Jesus, king of the Jews**. To me on the outside of religion, it sounds more like their **devil, Satan** himself, the one that reportedly **kills the innocent**. *If I were a Christian, I would not want this killer El Nino/Jesus Christ associated with any of my good and loving gods.*

Could there be a reason the translated word 'El Nino' from Spanish to English never happened? Think of what I am saying,,, if the

weather man reported that a big weather change causing fires to spread, droughts, famine, heat waves, tornados and death, were named for the son of god,,, the Christ Child,,, would people follow his teachings or would they leave the catholic church?

Regardless, this **Christ Child** or **El Nino** or **Blob,** is caused by the water in the largest ocean on the planet, heating up. Is this something you think can be fixed? Remember, there is less and less ICE on the planet every day to cool us down. *It is going to get very hot,,, very soon! How do you prepare for this future?*

December 30, 2015

Now remember, this is the middle of winter, the North Pole should be frozen over, and yet per this report, a deep low pressure area moved over Iceland and brought hurricane force winds,,, **bringing warm air**. Temperatures at the North Pole rose above the freezing point for the first time on record. And yet silence from the masses of all life as we march ever closer to the end.

All this in spite of Mother Nature screaming at the top of her lungs, warning us that Nature's Rights and its Laws are about to be implemented upon us all. There is not much time left.

The **Christ Child El Nino** is (or was) a prolonged warming phase of a band of ocean water developing in the central part of the Pacific Ocean, sometimes called ENSO. This lasts (normally) about 3 months, however when oceans cannot cool down normally, it is going to remain warm and become that much easier to heat up the following year. That is the path (setting new heat records) we are all on. How will that look in the future? What path are we on and how is it to turn out for all of us here on the ever warming once blue planet?

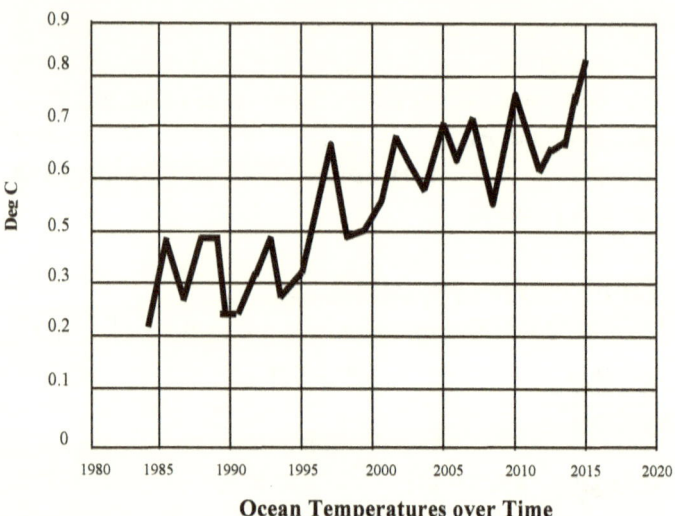

Ocean Temperatures over Time

The ice on the North Pole took approximately 2.7 million years to build up, giving us all a mild climate in which to live and in less than 100 years we have caused this vast space of water not to freeze over for the first time the winter of 2015-2016. *This is very bad for the future of the planet and clearly shows us all,,, it is going to get a lot hotter a lot quicker than originally thought.*

For those of you that don't get it, the sun and its heat, deflect off the ice helping keep us all cooler. The man made air pollution falls upon the ice, making it melt faster and faster. With no ice, the sun is able to move into the dark deep waters of the north and helps speed up the heating of the planet. This melting and heating is going to happen much faster than predicted and only the ones that prepare will survive.

Who will the people be that will live and who will be the ones to starve for lack of food and water. Is that what the FEMA Death Camps are for,,, to postpone the inevitable future? Did they pick out good places or bad ones? The answer is,,, bad ones. *North America is not a place you want to be in the next 50 years, as everything is going to get **very** hot.*

Straw Houses

February 9, 2015

In the growing need to build new homes for the ever growing populations of the world, straw houses are not only being considered feasible, but are under construction in the UK. *I am not making this up,,, you can go there and buy one.*

These **"Environmentally Friendly Homes"** will cost less, be well insulated and per the proponents or builders, earthquake proof, to some extent. The only drawback is, hay fever, cows, horse, mice, rats, birds, wind, decay and fire. Otherwise this is a real good idea.

*Oh yeah,,, **sign me up**. We know this is a good idea because there are so many ancient straw houses that have survived the test of time. Oh* *wait,,, there's none.* **Insanity has taken over in the form of,,, make it cheaper so we can make more money.** *The only ones that will be hurt will be the ones buying into this, believing governments will do the right thing for them, when we all know that they won't.*

Ignorance of man and his temporary solutions to the population explosion

Sand Mafia

It has been known for a long time now, that construction drives an economy,,, as well as printing money with no value (God/Notes). Construction is an artificial high that governments love and as we all know, are addicted to. Every country is fanning the flames of growth at this time regardless of the outcome to the environment. *To most countries that I see, there is no environmental concern, just **god/notes** to be made and of course,,, spent as fast as they can, while they still have value.*

Countries like Russia, China and India have adopted this, the American model of growth,,, or the American Dream,,, and away we go without a care of the Earth and its future. China has built many highways to nowhere and new countless empty cities. The buildings are too expensive for the people that built them to buy and live in. The sad part is, as I understand, 30% of the world's new constructions are sitting empty. *At what point does this global bubble burst,,, 50% vacancy? What in the big mix of things will bring this all crashing down? Whatever it will be,,, know it is going to happen and when it does,,, where will you be financially?*

Not to digress from sand but construction is the use of sand and the following is a chart to show the over-building bubble:

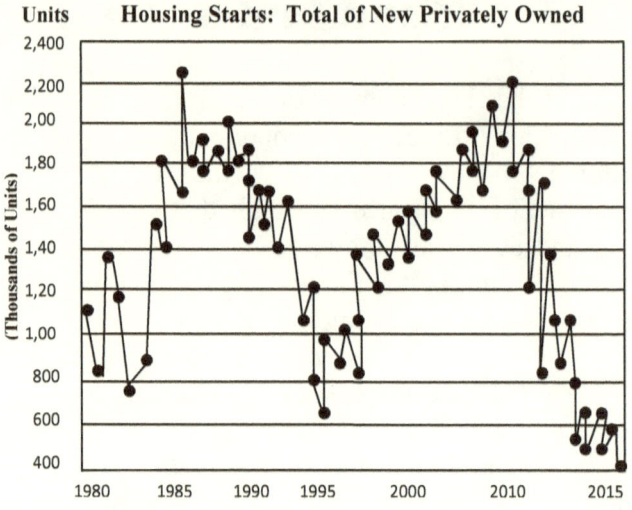

Construction sand is heavy and expensive to move so builders try to find **local sand,,,** even if it is illegal to mine,,, like parks and beaches. So where there is a need for sand, the **Sand Mafia** will fill that need. *I don't know why, but dirt always rises to the top. Why is doing the right thing,,, so hard to do for humans? Oh yeah,,, money,,, the quest for the god/notes at any price.*

A beach draws people and all that sand requires hotels and restaurants to house and feed the coming masses so as to make money. Construction is started and the need for construction material like sand,,, is right at their feet,,, so there is no need to ship in any and so they don't.

Now I am not making this up. The builders (outside the United States) in pursuit of the almighty dollar or **god/notes** take all the sand from the beach around them and build a building with it.

Now the sand that drew the people is gone and the sand that once was on the beach full of salt is now wrapping iron supports that make up the building. The salt eats away at the iron supports and the buildings are soon to be coming down via gravity.

This discarded rubble will lie on craggy rocks left by the sand thieves. Where once there were soft beautiful sandy beaches, full of life, for miles – instead, miles of craggy rocks and rubble are all that remain. *Death and destruction, it would seem, is a trademark of man's **ignorance and greed** and just can't be avoided. Even though each one knows what they are doing is wrong,,, they each do it anyway for self enrichment,,, **god notes**.*

The Sand Thieves now cross the globe taking what is just under the surface of the water with ships that are designed to suck up sand from just under the surface of the sea,,, **near your beach**. You don't even know it is gone until you don't see the sand anymore.

The construction industry uses the stolen sand for concrete and bricks and making all those black top roads covering the planet. They can't use desert sand for it is rounded and not jagged where it will bond.

Another man-made disaster unfolding in front of our eyes and we say and do nothing.

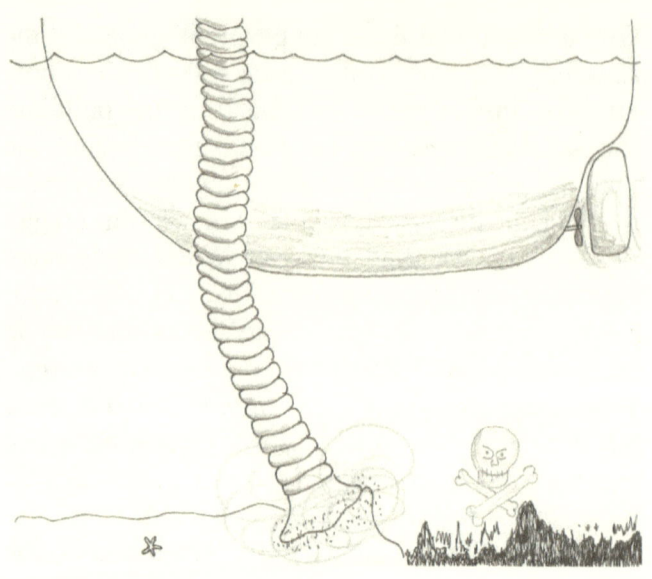

Coastal Erosion

Reportedly, Louisiana has lost 1,500 square miles of wetlands since 1930 and we are only getting started. This is land turned to sea in under 90 years. This is, or was land habitat production for sea food (30% of American production) turned to open water. Without the land, the oil industry pipes are exposed and storms like hurricanes will have new disastrous effects. Thousands of miles of pipes are now exposed to salt and wave actions soon will be breaking them open spewing out new black muck most likely killing what is left.

It is estimated that by the year 2020 a full one third of the state will become water and the lost seafood will be gone for good. What will people eat when **this** food source is no more?

Nature's Rights

Now this is another one to pay attention to, for it is about not only land but once more,,, food. Nature's Rights or laws for all living things. Some new form of Life,,, may prevail as it will become necessary to eliminate the reckless cause of death and destruction,,, man, so other forms of life may live and enjoy the gift of life,,, without god and paper money.

It should be clear to anyone that the erosion will continue and as sea levels rise, there will be massive land loss in this part of our country. We are at a point where miles of land loss could occur in one storm.

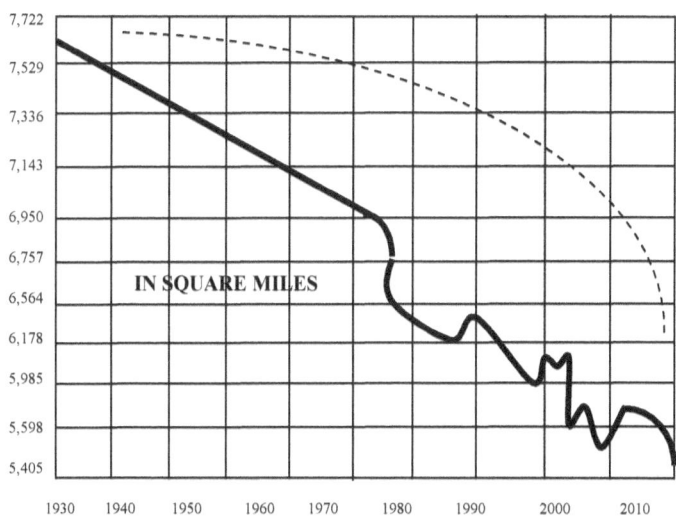

COASTAL LOUISIANA LAND AREA DECREASING

----- **From 1932 – 2010 1,883 sq. Miles Gone**

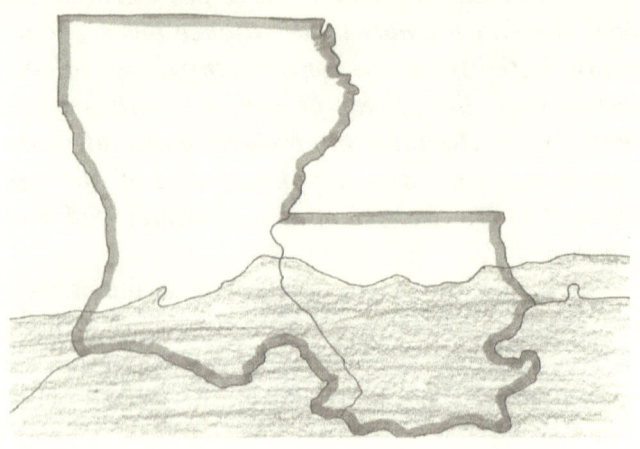

State of Louisiana soon to be under water.

"Godzilla Weather Patterns"

August 15, 2015

The National Weather Service reported that a "**Godzilla El Nino**" (*don't you just love these names?*) is growing in the Pacific Ocean and they predict a powerful weather change bringing much needed rain to the western part of the United States. (It should be noted by the end of 2016 they did not get any of this predicted rain.) This is the same people that predicted, ten years ago, an increase in hurricanes in the Atlantic Ocean that would bring much destruction to the eastern part of America,,, that did not happen.

They are not to be believed or trusted because they truly don't know what they are talking about,,, and this is their business,,, or they are told to lie to the masses. **As I said before,,, this is about the damage done to the air.**

What makes an El Nino? Hot water makes it - a lot of hot water. Lots of hot water make Hurricanes. What happened to all the hurricanes they,,, the experts,,, predicted? There may be a reduction of atmosphere because man has converted air into God/Notes and toxins.

Hurricanes

What makes hurricanes? Hot water and a lot of it! So what happened to all the hurricanes the expert predicted? They said it was going to happen,,, based on their science,,, so why did it not happen,,, what did they miss? **Remember those questions**. Why have we had several very mild years in a row if the oceans are getting hotter each year? *Now this is the point to a major problem facing us and I hope you do not speed read through this.*

How could the predictors of the weather,,, the ones that study this every day,,, get it so wrong and then not tell us why? What is there in the mix facing us all that is missing, that now **prevents** the predicted Hurricanes from happening? What is there in the mix that is now,,, not there,,, or has been added that prevents hurricanes from happening? If we pick apart a hurricane, we know we need hot open water, evaporated water, wind and oh yes, **air**. We have all of that don't we? See Chapter 4 on air.

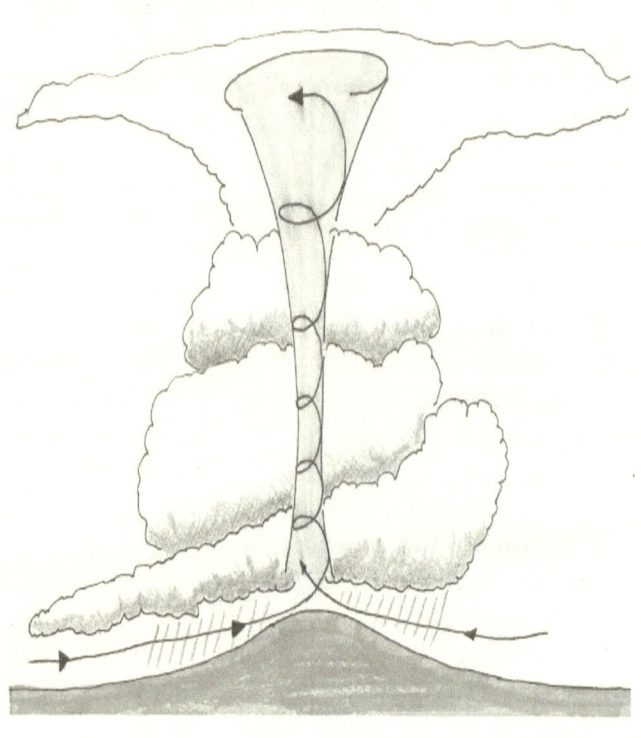

Normal hurricane before 1950's when they were massive

The following is a chart showing decrease in named hurricanes.

Year	Named Storms	Hurricanes	Major Hurricanes
2015	3	0	0
2013	14	2	0
2011	18	6	3
2009	9	3	2
2007	15	5	2
2005	28	15	7
2003	16	7	3
2001	15	9	4
1999	12	8	5
1996	13	9	6
1994	7	3	0
1992	7	4	1
1990	14	8	1
1988	12	5	3
1985	11	7	3
1983	4	3	1
1980	11	9	3

It should be noted that a named storm does not mean a powerful storm. Over the past decade these storms have had next to no punch,,, why?

**Decreasing Tropical Storms Due to Global Warming
Less Air to Feed the Storms**

The Next Global Weather Changes and Droughts

Are you ready?

March 19, 2015

The National Oceanic and Atmospheric Administration or NOAA announced that 2014 was the "warmest year on record" and yet some of the eastern part of the United States had record cold temperatures in the year 2014. *They still don't offer an explanation as to why,,, but I think I have shown what is causing this..*

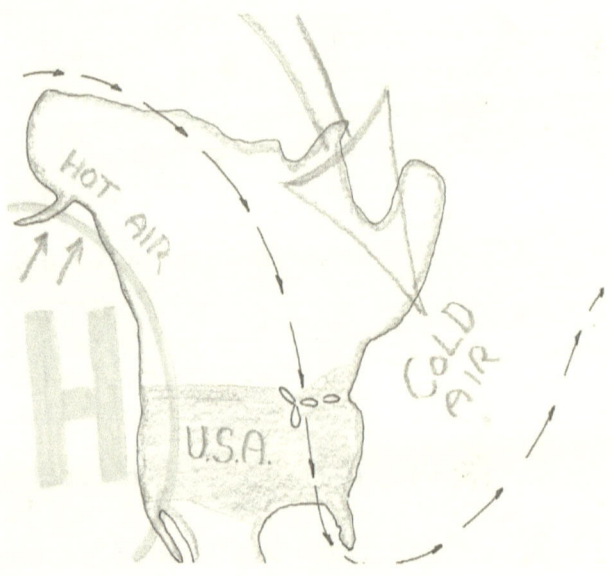

High pressure in the Pacific Ocean is pushing hot air up into Canada. Thereby pushing cold air down into the Eastern part of the U.S.A. causing the illusion that everything is fine,,, but its not.

April 14, 2015

Reportedly, the warming or heating up of the Pacific Ocean is causing a ripple in the Jet Stream and that ripple circles the planet in waves. This new pattern is now being pushed off course to create a ripple effect or pattern (from the Pacific Ocean) that shoves hot air up north (Alaska) and that in turn pushes cold air south (east coast of North America). That is why we had, a cooler winter and still had a cool summer in the eastern part of the United States and drought and heat in the western part. Alaska is experiencing temperatures over 14 degrees above normal and this is only going to continue.

However, this ripple in the jet stream is far reaching and is changing weather all across the upper part of this planet. In 2013, the **hot spot** was in Russia and that carried over into 2014 moving from Europe down into China.

*The term **Hot Spot** means; a hole in the lower air (thicker air) that permits the effects of the sun to come to earth and take us into super heating. A hole in the lower air The Hot Spot is showing us all the future and it is going to get hotter as these holes start to pop up across the globe.*

April 23, 2015

It was reported that with the arrival of summer this year, Alaska was having unseasonable warmth and a large snow melt. Some places having rain instead of snow and others having neither that have led to a heightened wildfire risk. Other parts are under water restrictions and a partial drought.

As you can see the changes are coming at us very fast and there just is not time to wonder if these changes are real. **I can assure you, they are real and you need to prepare,,, for Nature's Rights will prevail and we don't even understand the laws (cause and effect) yet.** *But you can see,,, if we don't have air to permit rain,,, it will be bad.*

Image of the future most of us will not see

May 7, 2015

Tornado hits Butzow and Hamburg Germany. Man stated "I have never seen anything like this in my life." This is new weather for Europe and more to come, via man's ignorance and greed.

June 5, 2015

UK reports the "Hottest July Day" on record. Hot weather may have been a contributing factor to a large fire consuming about 30 acres of forest.

August 15, 2015

Travel alerts,,, 'check your destination if you are planning a River Cruise in a foreign country'. They may not have the water to float a boat. The Rhine River in Germany reports that the tour boats are sitting on the river bed,,, in mud. No water in the river. Farmers are worried about what is going to happen to their crops,,, with no water.

This is not just a local problem but a global one that will be facing us all every day, very soon.

December 31, 2015

Storm Frank brought temperatures 20 degrees above normal and caused flooding across Ireland.

January 10, 2016

Arctic Snow bomb smashes into Britain bringing with it the coldest winter in 58 years. Hot air up from Pacific Ocean pushes cold air down as part of the ripple. *These cold waves will not happen many more times in the future, for what makes cold air is melting away. If the ice is gone,,, so are the winters.* **This is to be a short lived event as all the ice will be gone in under 20 years and most likely in 10. There will be no more winters in the north of our planet,,, just hotter summers with less rain. The last of the ice will be gone approximately between 2025 and 2030.**

The Bottom Half

Australia and Indonesia are also heating up; there are reports of record fires. Tiny Indonesia is coming up on top as the greatest producer of carbon air pollution in the world in the year 2014.

China is number one as America sends jobs overseas along with the American Dream. In second place is the United States at about half as much pollution; then comes the European Union (consisting of 28 countries). Indonesia falls per one report, at 12th out of all the polluters in the world. *See America is starting to lag behind China in the consumption of air.*

As Indonesia's forest burn in the hopes of growing (**god/notes**) more food to sell, the water down under is also heating up and they have Typhoons of enormous size and strength. The southern part of our world is experiencing stronger storms, because their air down under is thicker. The two masses of air are separated by the motion of the earth as it creates vortexes and jet streams that are separated from each other.

Total Storms	Year	Tropical Storms	Typhoons	Super Typhoons
39	1964	13	19	7
35	1965	14	10	11
	1967	15	16	4
	1971	11	16	4
34	1994	14	14	6
33	1996	12	15	6
32	1974	16	16	0
31	1989	10	15	6
	1992	9	17	5
30	1962	7	17	6
	1966	10	17	3
	1972	8	20	2
	1990	9	17	4
	2004	10	13	7
	2013	17	8	5

Tropical Storms from 1962 -2013

Now you can see. In the north side of the planet we are having less or no hurricanes when we use to have many of them every year and they were very powerful.

Those that understand how storms normally are made know there must be more storms and they will be stronger. The equation seems to work below the equator,,, but it is not working up north? What frightening part is missing in the weather wizards' ability to predict the future? **AIR!** *Remember that question because at this time no one is talking about this,,, no one!*

Nature's Rights

Chapter Four

Air
Or
Lack There Of

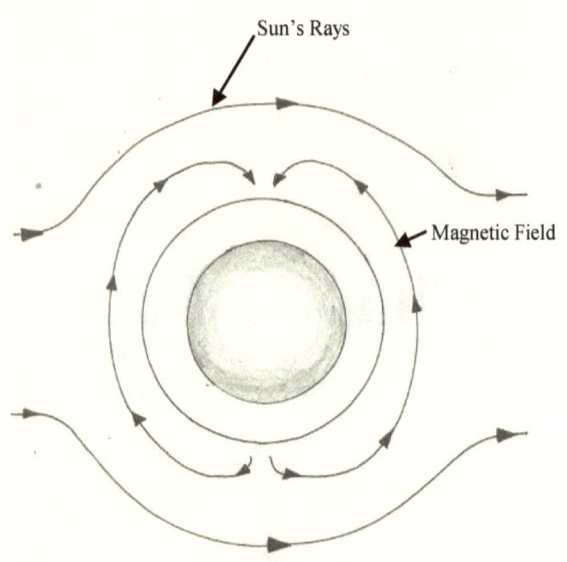

Sun's Rays

Magnetic Field

Earth

$\mathbf{T}$his chapter summarizes Global Warming to some extent and the full effects of man on this planet and the end result of his relentless greed for **god/notes**. This chapter for most will be hard to look at and yet will show beyond any doubt that the crash is coming and it will be very bad. I will start at what I believe is critical for us all to understand and that is life giving **AIR**. Is a life giving breathable gas being turned in to a deadly acid and disappearing as it is converted into poison before our eyes and within four generations?

Air reportedly is a mixture of gases, 78% nitrogen and 21% oxygen with traces of water vapor $H2O$ and a mixed bag of other regional components, some toxic. This mixed bag of gases took hundreds of millions of years to build up and now is being consumed or turned into carbon dioxide at record speeds. **Carbon dioxide is toxic to animal life,,, that would include us.**

The earth has a magnetic field surrounding it (magma and particles emanating as a constant stream) that prevents the solar winds from the sun pushing the air out into space. This permits air to accumulate on this planet. So at the beginning of this planet's life it could keep the oxygen produced here on earth, permitting life to grow.

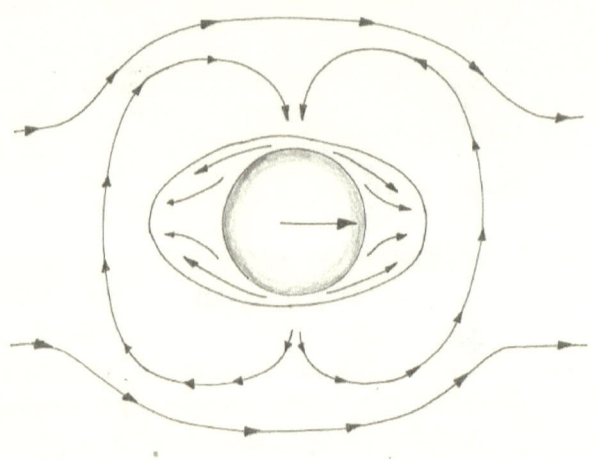

Earth and the centrifugal force in the atmosphere

The sun shines down on the earth (energy), the plants consume carbon dioxide (also producing sugar), and change CO_2 to oxygen O_2 and this is called **Photosynthesis**. Sometimes referred to as the **Carbon Cycle** and for me, we humans live on the wastes or excesses of all plants. Man is a parasite.

Plants need oxygen and produce it at ten times their needs, because in the beginning of life here on this planet there was none to be found, so they had to grow their own (self contained). To ensure they had enough, they made too much. Excess oxygen from plants, was released and over time created an atmosphere that other life could take advantage of. The oldest plants found are over 400 million years old. As time went on and air (oxygen) supplies grew,,, because nothing was using this excess, consuming it, destroying it, or converting it to acid, it became plentiful. That is until man came along perusing **god/notes**.

Now keep in mind,,, it took millions of years to accumulate miles of air surrounding the planet,,, and we all are recklessly burning through it in just a few life times.

The outer limits of the layer of atmospheric gases, commonly called air is at about 62 miles or 327,360 feet or 100 km. This outer edge is called the Karman Line. **All that we know that is living within the universe is within this thin space. From the core or magma to the outer ring of air,,, we are it and look at what we are doing to it.**

Now most of us who are older have heard the pilot announce to the passengers of a jet, "We are going to be cruising at 39,000 feet." May be that is because I have not been in a plane for a long time (30 years), and those announced levels have been dropping.

Now the following is important so please <u>do not speed read this</u>. Stop and read these words for full comprehension.

In a news report in August of 2015, they announced a European commercial flight was at 36,000 feet when it suddenly stalled out and dove to 7,000 before the pilot could restart the engines. When I looked up this news report,,, the next day,,, there was nothing. Not a word on this flight. As I remember the announcer went on to say, *(I think it was the equivalent to our FAA European Aviation Safety Agency,,, EASA) told them (the pilots) that,* "They would have to fly at 28,000 feet from now on." Now the information is from memory and not confirmed for there is no written report that I can find (not normal).

For the record, 39,000 feet is about 7 miles and 20,000 feet is about 4 miles. You can walk 3.1 miles in one hour. So if we could walk to the end of abundant air, it would take about four hours. That is all the height of the air we have for all of us. *And that air is disappearing at an alarming rate. No one is talking about it,,, no one,,, and most likely they never will, until it is to late or planes start falling from the sky more often. This is called tombstone mentality and in aviation air safety, it takes dead bodies before defects will be changed, most times not even then.*

The concentrations (volume) of oxygen have been dropping at an alarming rate and we just don't want to talk about it. Those in the know are stating the oxygen levels 100,000 years ago, were higher than today's levels. The disturbing part is (as I understand and interpret it) since the industrial revolution we on this planet have seen a reduction of our air by fully one third. 1/3... gone. **Where did it go?**

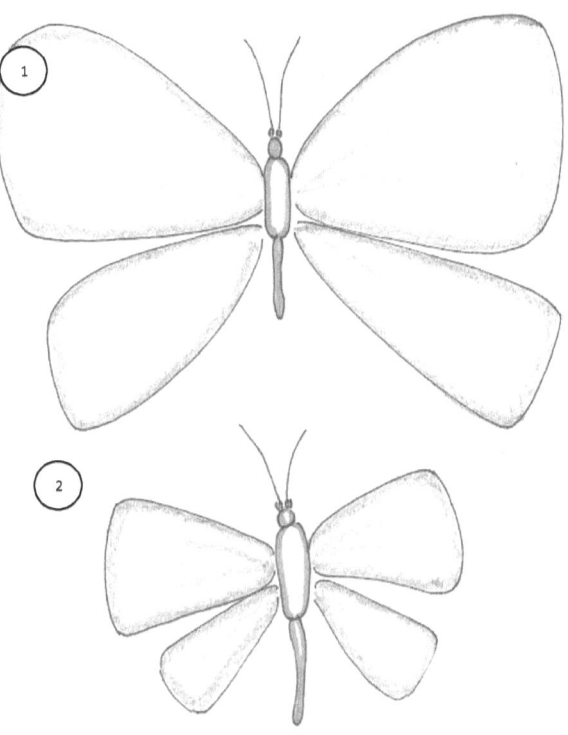

Above is an image of an extinct species of butterfly from 100,000 years ago. Note that the body is the same size as present day butterflies, but the wings are smaller. Present butterflies require larger wings in order to fly.

The Rise and fall in CO2 Levels between 1990 - 2008

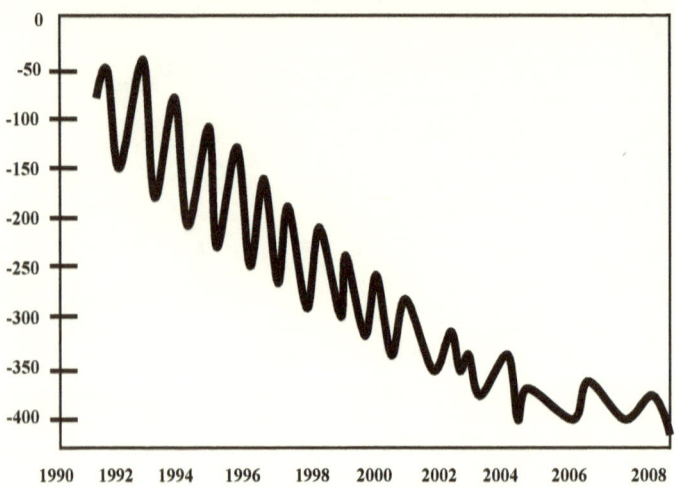

1/3 in 150 years.

Some major cities in the world are experiencing (allegedly) a drop in oxygen up to 50%. These people clearly never saw any of the images coming from China's big cities where they must be running on 10% or less. ***The air is almost black with cancer causing pollution.***

It is reported by the CDC (Centers for Disease Control) that the first decade of this century, reportedly saw the number of Asthmatic patients increase over 25%,,, in just ten years. It is estimated that in 2001, 1 in 12 people had Asthma and in 2009, 1 in 14 have this affliction. Now, it should also be noted that among non white children, they show a 50% increase in that same time. Once more, that is in just 10 years and I wonder, is it the lack of oxygen or what we are putting in the air, or converting the air it to? See Global Shading in Chapter 5.

The elevation of Asthma among blacks is much worse than among white's. I wonder is it because our history is found on two different climates? Historically, white people from thinner colder climates show a lower increase in asthma and black people in thicker warmer climates show a higher increase in this affliction.

One proponent of, 'Everything Is Fine,' say the trees that produce air have been cut down and now **they produce less air every year** (implying the air gets replaced each year) and that is why we have less air today. To them I say, it must have taken millions of years to produce this air we are going through in just over one hundred years,,, idiot!!!

We humans are turning good clean air into carbon dioxide (acid), that is dumping into the oceans killing off the sea life, coral reef and shell creatures,,, or our food. The chemical air has now been converted into something else. That air that once was and took millions of years to accumulate, is now gone! Air is converted in to death. Asthma is the first sign of what is to come and come in a big way for all of us.

Chemicals in Our Homes

The chemical industry is doing just fine as it helps pass laws (by buying politicians) to force the public to use their manufactured products (like Obama health care,,, it's the law). That new couch you just bought is made with chemicals that make them fire resistant. Only thing is, it also fills the air in your home with toxins that cause cancer. The fibers come loose, are breathed in to our lungs or fall on the floor and become cancer causing dust bunnies that drift about our home and end up in our food and our lungs and in turn our blood.

These chemicals are in everything from our curtains and carpet to other upholstered furniture; and when they burn in a house fire they give off extremely toxic chemical gases that kill before the fire. The solution would seem to be, don't buy new curtains, carpet or upholstered furniture. Have tile floors, use blinds or make the curtains yourself and/or have them made as you would do when you reupholster your furniture with chemical free coverings.

Radiation

October 21, 2015

There are unseen dangers all around us and one is government. Reportedly there are 24 sites in 10 states that have what is called low-level radioactive contamination. This is not including the high level radioactive material some held at power plants near you.

This radioactive material can take from 2000 to 5000 years to become safe once more,,, we just don't have that much time. The crash of the global god/notes will see this cross the globe as part of the 6th die off, just for us.

It would seem that radioactive material manufacturing plants in these states, now long gone, have left several Active Cleanup Sites. You and I pay the price (or our children or grand children) for cheap power as the ones that did make the mess get away with all the **god/notes**.

Please note the following global map does not include military nuclear power plants and their pretense of nuclear waste storage.

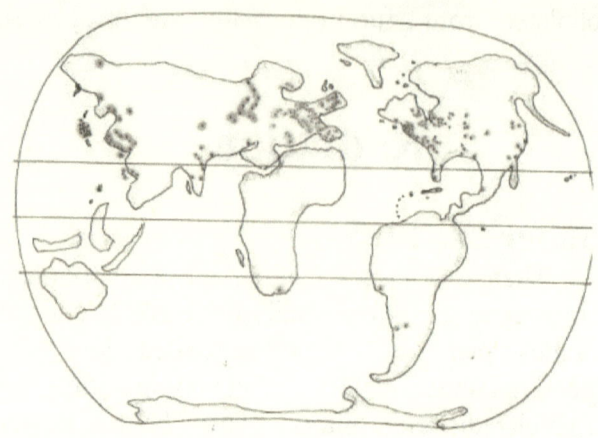

Known locations of nuclear power plants around the world.

Maybe it was not so cheap after all,,, and think of all the power plants across the planet. When there is not money (crash of **god/notes**) to clean them up after their estimated life span of 30 to 40 years,,, how will this be contained,,, it will not,,, that is how.

Over 75% of these power plants are at the end of their life span and are due to close because of contamination. This is going to hit in the next 10 years.

October 29, 2015

West Lake Landfill is found in Missouri and consists of three dumps. Two are radioactive and one is just trash. The trash dump is on fire and has been **burning for years** and the fear is the radioactive dump is leaking into the ground water and air. **They who made the radioactive waste are long gone with their god/notes.**

Due to the discovery of radioactive and other contaminants at the dump site, (they just discovered this) it was proposed as a superfund site in 1989 and still is a mess. *It should be clear,,, like education,,, no amount of money is going to fix this. This is one of thousands of sites that will be a mess for thousands of years as radioactivity spreads across the globe.*

Most Disturbing

There is currently reports of underground,,, under the Ogallala Aquifer,,, harvesting of radioactive material for the nuclear power industry. Whereby, they use **toxic chemicals** to remove **most** of the radioactive material. The toxic chemicals and uncollected radioactive material is now leaching back into the Ogallala Aquifer that covers much of the Midwest of the United States and then exchanged for God/Notes. **How can this be good for America? Unless you look at corporate America.**

This radioactive matter is now coming out in people's wells and they cannot drink it, bathe in it, feed it to their animals, water the grass or grow food with it. This water system is a major producer of food for much of the United States.

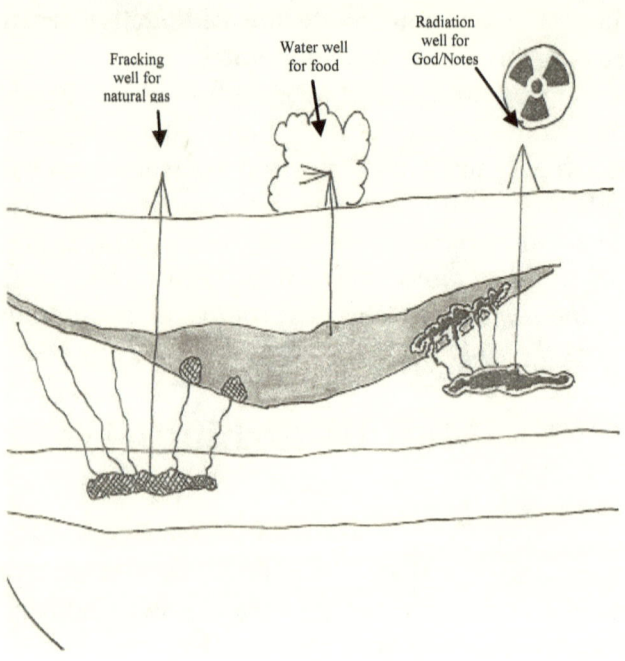

A better life through chemicals?? I don't think so.

The future should be clear to all of us that we,,, man is to adjust to living with these chemicals, left by the Deceivers and money takers. The good days are over and long gone and our children will have to face our naivety for trusting the bought and paid for politicians that live like kings.

The time of the end of the Ogallala Aquifer

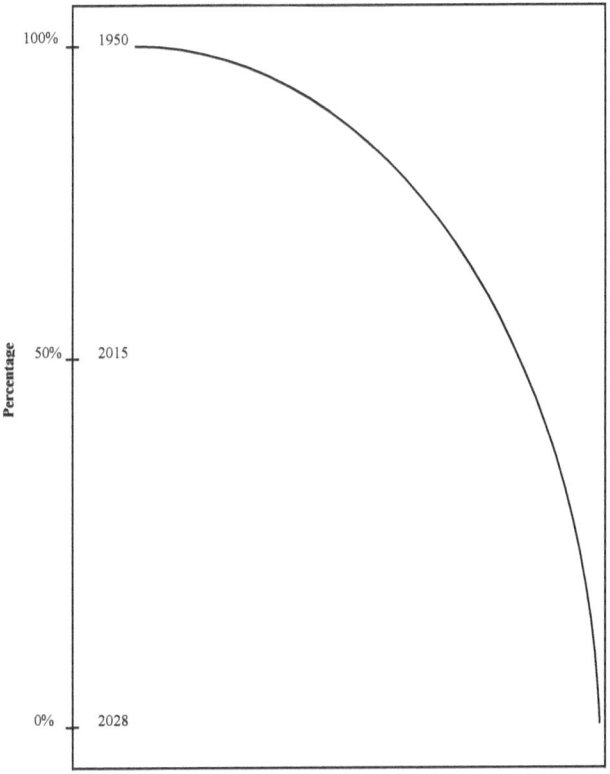

(This is an estimate only by the Author)

Nature's Rights

Chapter Five

Global Shading

**Image of the future of Earth after
Global Financial Super Heating**

Nature's Rights

Right after 911, there was a report that came out called **Global Shading** around 2002, and to this date I cannot find any information on it from the original report. I would like to give the creator or discoverer credit for his work, but cannot find his name, so I will call him Mr. X. It is as though the government does not want anyone to know him or his work. Perhaps they fear the retribution that accompanies transference.

The theory goes like this,,, Mr. X believes long before 911 that the planet was being artificially cooled by the jet planes contrails (chemical trails) in the upper atmosphere producing miniscule particles of air pollution that stayed in the upper atmosphere for long periods reflecting the sun's rays, but he could not prove it. Most people thought he was nuts and dismissed him and his theory, **as they still do to this very day**. Then came that horrible day,, 911 when Saudi revenge (read Jesus Christ in Canaan) woke up America to the modern day Christian Crusade. It was another war over god; for power and/or oil and their almighty **god/notes**.

As the story goes, on the next day (9-12) Mr. X realized this was his moment. So called all his friends around the world and asked them to track the air, ground and water temperatures. Over the next days, while George W. Bush had ordered all planes grounded,,, the end result was,,, **overall planet temperature rose by 1.5 degrees,,, in only three days**.

Now you can find reports on **Global Dimming** (not Global Shading), where less sunlight is hitting the earth due to manmade visible air pollution. Allegedly this pollution reflects the sunlight, *would not that be the same thing? What happened to Mr. X? Maybe I am just not that good at finding things,,, but he is out there.*

Per the proponents of this **Global Dimming** it is estimated to have had a worldwide temperature reduction over the past years of reportedly 5%. *Is not that the same thing?* Man is creating pollutions that are preventing the full effects of global warming,,, all for the almighty **god/note.** Whatever you want to call it, the upper atmospheric pollution is keeping us cooler, (for a short time) while the lower pollution is trapping heat and melting ice, continuing to heat things up even faster.

Now moving from 2001 to 2009 Global Shading has disappeared as non-science. There are new reports of the government allegedly dumping chemicals into the upper atmosphere. *This is what I call their silver bullet mentality. They believe more pollution is the answer to more pollution. You can bet,,, someone is making money.* Reportedly, airlines are paid to dump toxins (aerosols) into our air for us to breathe, but with what effect?

1. Deflects upper atmosphere sun's rays that heat up the surface of the planet. **That is good.**
2. This new pollution helps to trap heat in the lower atmosphere, helping to heat up the planet even faster. **That is bad.**
3. Dirt from jets land on the ice on the North and South Poles melting the ice quicker. **That is bad.**
4. Asthma has unexplained growth,,, until now. **That is bad.**
5. These new pollutants are being dumped into the air, allegedly causing these new levels of asthma, and may in fact cause new types of lung cancer. **That is bad**. But good for the medical industry.

It would seem the federal government always does the wrong things first, (because they take bribes) then when it must, (the crooks) will do the right thing,,, but only when they are caught and must. The full effects of this prolonged slow death of the life on earth is unfolding before our eyes if only people will open them to see,,, the future is here,,, now,,, right before us and it is very bad.

Space Sun Shade

November 2006

Now I am not making this up and I can't believe we are so resistant to giving up fossil fuels to enrich the 1%ers. **Space Sunshade** is called a type of radiation management. These space people believe they can erect a sunshield between earth and the sun to shade the planet as Global Warming continues its endless path of death.

To me it would be easier to fix the problem of pollution or our reliance on fossil fuels,,, but not when we are dealing with the greed factor of the ***god/note*** *people.*

These people want to assemble a sun shade between the sun and earth, no kidding, twenty million tons of more space debris so we can keep consuming what is left of the air (converting it to toxins) and un-renewable power resources (oil) and of course make more **god/notes** for themselves.

I wonder just how much oxygen it will take to push 20 million tons of metal and/or plastic up into space, creating more pollution for all of us to breathe. This is why I believe we will see more asthma and allergies (allergic reactions to foreign man made toxic particles man has mixed into the air). As these toxins enter our bodies, what new ailments are to come to enrich the doctors and criminal drug industries that now make and sell opiates, killing an estimated 76 people ever day in America, as of 2015? The **god/notes** and greed or the perception of their value are what is killing everything. *Religion and god/notes... perceptions of man,,, running head long into Nature's Rights and its laws we have yet to fully understand,,, but will at one point have it shown to us, when it is too late.*

The real question is how much air will it use up to make this shade out in space and all those **god/notes**?

The goal of this insane idea is beyond my logic to comprehend, but they (the inventers of this mad idea) believe a **Space Sunshade** will net the planet a 2% reduction in deflecting sunlight. If asked, I would not take the time to write such a ludicrous concept on paper (waste of time and paper) and yet, these idiots did. There proposal is to build large Rail guns or Coil guns, firing a capsule containing a million shades into space every five minutes,,, for 10 years,,, from 20 launch sites. That is one every 30 seconds for 10 years,,, to get just 2%. Now someone has to be out there to catch these capsules coming every 30 seconds, 24 hours per day for 10 years and those people,,, these army people or robots would still have to assemble all the shades, and that they estimate will take 50 years. They really think this will stop global warming; but at what expense? How much air will they use and how much more pollution will it create increasing the earth's temperature? I estimate the costs will outweigh the benefits long before it is ever completed.

The average ocean temperature is 62.6 degrees. The average air temperature between the years of 1951–1980 was 57.2 degrees globally. In 2015, the temperature was about 1.8 degrees warmer, topping out to about 59 degrees.

The average land temperature as of 2015 is 1.62 degrees above the 20th century average of 57 degrees; making the new average about 59 degrees. Since 1976, every year including 2015 has had an average warming of 0.50 degrees per decade over land, an average warming of 0.22 degrees over ocean. By 2020, it is projected that global surface temperatures will be more than 0.9 degrees warmer than the 1986-2005 average of 57 degrees.

However, the projected temperature will likely be several degrees warmer if carbon-dioxide emissions are left unchecked. This means, as of

2015, the average land and water temps have risen 1.62 degrees, for a new average of 58.62 degrees.

If all the ice over the world melted, the sea would rise an estimated 216 feet, and the average temperature would change to about 80 degrees instead of the 58 degrees that it is today. Which will keep climbing to unbelievable levels,. The animal life that relies on the icy seas for food will either go extinct or find ways to adapt.

February 2015

Climate Engineering or Geo-engineering is where man, in an attempt to control the weather (with chemicals) and global warming, is dumping sulfur dioxide into the stratosphere. The plan is to use jumbo jets to dump "scatterers" and deflect the sun's rays (Global Shading).

The only drawback is these pollutants will have unknown dangers and long range effects on those that rely on clean air to breathe. Don't these chemicals cause acid-rain that is now going into our lungs? If the pollutants cause acid when it hits water like rain what do you think it is doing when it hits your lungs; once more creating even more allergies and more asthma cases and lung cancer as we all suffocate to death.

Nature's Rights

Chapter Six

Water

Juice of the Stars

A simple system and yet we cannot fathom it and our place within the design.

Nature's Rights

Water, as we all know, is one of the key ingredients of life; and like air, we cannot live without it. Yet, it would seem to mean so little to the governments we entrust with its care. It seems to me, on the outside, that people in government are more interested in getting other people fired, moving up some sort of a ladder made of self importance, grandeur, power, influence and of course money or **god/notes**. When they get to the top, any top will do, their dream job, (power for sale), they seem to shuffle papers, give speeches and make excuses,,, while building golden parachutes.

For me, I see all water as Life Giving and it should be respected, for it is the **Juice of the Stars** and very rare. When you add all the necessary elements together to build life, we as humans seem to be trying our best to destroy it as fast as we can. I don't understand the race to kill everything, but it has something to do with education (or lack thereof) and greed, **god/notes**. I would add God and all religions, for the "go forth, be fruitful and multiply" thing undoubtedly has not helped and in fact had a devastating effect on this planet. The man made religious plague, this mental disorder called **Scrupulosity** is to share in the responsibility and those of us on the outside of the God thing that say nothing.

It would seem all religions just do not care about the planet and the life on it. Collectively their concerns would lie in a place just out of sight, past the stars above and they will do anything to get there... anything. It would seem the great spaceship in the sky is the true goal of these religious people and their plan would seem to be,,, God can clean up the mess left behind by all of them. After all, it only took God 6 days to make the whole universe. *I think it will be the meek that clean it all up, long after they start to grow some balls and stand up to all the religious insanity.*

Wars over religious principles have turned into wars over the gods, (global religious domination) power (oil) and money, (**god/notes**). The next wars coming up will be over food and then water. Brother is today killing brother over the juice of the stars as we all keep our eyes on the true goal, (per the religious) heaven.

Sad to think we are given such a gift (life) and its experience and then we take no precautions to protect it and preserve it for the next souls. Life has such little value compared to the imaginary gods and all these imaginary heavens, which are the only goals of the earthbound holies whose goals are to be attained at any cost by the Deceivers. *We all know where these people are going, a place called heaven, and for many of us, in the next life, it is **the*** *place to avoid at all cost, for it is full of the hateful, lying, righteous, killing god people.   Who would want to spend five minutes with these nut jobs,,, let alone all of eternity? I will pass. Heaven is a place to be avoided at all costs.*

The list of polluted waterways in the world is too long to list, for there is no body of water on this planet that is free of cancer causing heavy metals.   But I would like to hit on a few that will affect our future.   The health of our water is long overdue, for a real concern will hit us all very soon as clean drinking water is rapidly disappearing before our eyes,,, and we do nothing and say nothing while others pollute it for **god/notes**.

August 5, 2015

The news is full of the EPA allegedly digging up the back side of an abandoned gold mine called Gold King Mine, dug in the gold rush of the 1920's.   Reportedly, the EPA dumped an estimated one million gallons of waste water (sludge), and then it was reported as three million gallons into the relatively clean Colorado River.

It was reported that there are thousands of these abandoned gold minds and that is not to mention the death, waiting for us at Leadville Colorado.   The money (**god/notes**) was taken without regard for the land and the philosophy of **"let someone else pay to clean it up,"** worked well for them then, as it works well today.   They got the money, we got the mess.   *The bad thing is it cost more to clean it all up than all the money they made making the mess.*

If you live near this river, you should not eat the fish or drink the water, for these newly deposited toxins are now coating the rocks and river bed and can be reactivated at any stirring of the river beds surface,,, like heavy rain or spawning fish. *I would not eat the fish,,, if there are any left alive. And from the reports of toxins in the seas, I would avoid those fish as well (as I do).*

October 7, 2015

There are reports coming from Flint Michigan (a population of about 100 thousand people), that their **new water treatment plant** built to save money, (so they would not have to buy treated water, but use nearby river water) that this tap water is **full of LEAD!** Reportedly, this newly treated (contaminated) river water has been coming into homes for consumption for over a year and only at the end of September 2015, did the governor come out and acknowledge that **they have a problem**.

It is my understanding that the children of Flint have three times the level of lead in their systems than is considered safe. Lead poisoning stays in the human system for a long time and can cause brain defects (learning disabilities) as well as can kill. They are handing out free filters to remove the lead from the water,,, but do you really think the water is safe? *Would you drink this crap?*

The lead bits are apparently coming from the lead water pipes that are over 100 years old. As the **chemicals** (added at the new plant) used to purify the water are so caustic that they (the chemical) **will break down lead** and send it streaming into homes. Will these filters remove those water purifying chemicals that can dissolve lead? If it will dissolve lead,,, what is it doing to your stomach or liver or kidneys or your brain?

I am surprised the governor did not say, "Well you all should be grateful we are saving you money and the water is not that bad, its only lead... you can't burn it like you can in all the fracking communities. **One thing we know for sure is, we will not be told the truth by any one of these governments.**

Sinkholes

There are alarming numbers of these sinkholes appearing all across the world and it is presumed that the water being pumped out the ground is the cause. However, new studies show the **carbon dioxide** man put in the air and is now coming down as acid rain, is boring holes in the limestone. It is the combination of these two (acid rain - pumping quickly depleting drinking water) that is showing us our future. Less water to drink in our aquifers and that water is now polluted with **carbon dioxide**. *There is just no getting away from a future full of death from fossil fuel, god, religions and pursuit of the almighty* **god/notes**. *And I would add one more thing,,, apathy.*

The Black Sea

I just don't get this 'out of sight out of mind' thing in pursuit of the **god/note**, when we know the price to pay will be much worse down the road when so much wild life is gone. But we all should know by now that it is all about the money. The Black Sea has become a tourist trap and the need for new homes and new hotels has caused a building boom there.

Man can build the buildings but cannot build the infrastructure to support them. So all the waste goes under ground or in this case,,, into the sea,,, the Black Sea. The governments want the dollars and don't want to stand in the way, so just dump the sewage into the sea. *Out of sight, out of mind,,, let's all hurry and make the god/notes, as we treat all water on this planet as a toilet. This in not sustainable and there is a major price to pay, which is coming due very soon.*

The unique dolphins, natural to the Black Sea are dying off at an alarming rate. It is estimated in just a few years of mans greed, they will be gone for good. The Black Sea is soon to become Europe's newest Dead Sea and is the most polluted water in all of Europe. *Now that is not a nice record to hold. Only what drew people to this place is now polluted by the people that are drawn to this place.* **This is a massive amount of water and its end is less than 10 years.** *2025*

Polar Ice Melting

I remember watching a news report in the early 2000s, of how a man was trying to warn the federal government of the ice melting, specifically the North Pole. The president of the United States had a government agent in the room at the time of the interview to ensure that he did not say too much or the wrong things. **His words were controlled by this government and he and his knowledge of the truth was considered,,, a national security risk,,,** and he could not answer all the questions put to him. The president was George W. Bush. *In my view this man being interviewed, is just one of many that are* **political prisoners held within America. Freedom of Speech is not free in America**. *Knowledge is such a threat to those in power, the Deceivers. These guardians of the* **god/note,** *takers at this time would often say "There is no such thing as Global Warming,,, it is just the natural climate changes."* And we all blindly step in line.

The Polar Ice Sheets are reportedly melting much faster than first thought. **In the past 20 years this ice has melted more than in the past 10,000 years.** Satellite images of the North Pole show its reduction in size is at an accelerated rate. *It must be clear to you by now we just don't have much time left. My estimations are we have less than 10 years before it is* <u>all</u> *gone. 2025*

This polar sheet is estimated (by the Deceivers) to completely disappear by the year 2100 (85 years from now) at the northern tip of Greenland. And all that clean fresh drinking water will mix with the polluted non drinking salt water. I think it will happen much faster than they are reporting. *I put this closer to the year 2025 and it will be for the most part,,, all gone! That is when things will get hot for all of us, very hot.*

Northern Arctic Sea Ice Volume Projection

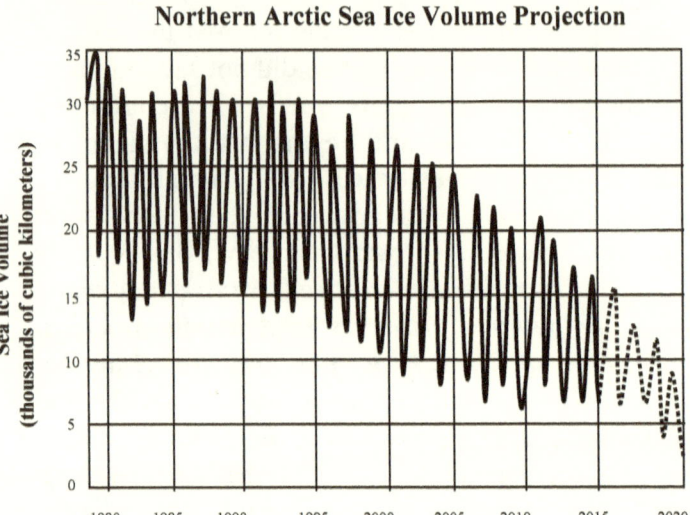

The year 2016 it was reported that the north pole did not freeze over for the first time,,, ever. The sun reflects off the white ice keeping the planet cooler. But if there is no ice to reflect off of,,, it will go straight in to the darker water and start heating it up as an accelerated rate. (**This is why I believe the melt down will be much faster.**) This will cause the water to heat up faster and cause the ice to milt faster. Their time line is off by over 80% in my estimation.

The man made Acid Rain being dumped into lakes and streams around the world also falls onto the North and South Pole, aiding in the disappearance of the ice. I am always taken back by how accustomed we humans can become to changes,,, (short memories) things like Acid Rain. Just so we all understand,,, that is ACID falling from the sky as RAIN, SNOW, FOG and DEW, ending up in our lakes, streams, rivers and glaciers,,, as well as our lungs and blood. We are drinking it and we are breathing it into our lungs. *It is killing us and our children. Oh yes,,, and what of our children?* **What is the next generation to see?**

DEATH!

May 11, 2015

The National Oceanic and Atmospheric Administration, stated in March of this year, 2015 was the warmest first quarter on record in the past 136 years of record taking.

They also believe **this melting** of global ice water is a "**long term trend**",,, *no kidding,,,* and accounts for 0.3 mm per year of ocean rise. *That is a lot of water when you spread it out all over the world.* Some estimates put the water level to be at 220 feet above today's levels when all the ice should melt. *Do you have any idea how hot this planet is going to be at that time? Air loss is the one thing no one is talking about. Converting clean air or our atmosphere into poison gas will be one more big part of the Sixth Die Off facing us all,,, as it aids in the great heating up and melt down of all the ice.*

161

Tampa Florida
Year 2100

May 16, 2015

The National Aeronautics and Space Administration states that in the year 2020 a 10,000 year old Antarctic ice shelf will disappear. This will most likely increase the pace of increasing sea levels. *When the ice is gone watch how fast the world temperature climbs. We will be living like rats in caves only coming out at night to feed like the Morlocks. Only this time it will not be an H. G. Wells science fiction, it will be the real thing.*

Drinking Water Destroyed By Gas Fracking Contamination

When we think we can safely dispose of oil and gas companies toxic wastewater by dumping it, under pressure, into the earth,,, well it is too late to rethink it. Hydraulic fracking, or another toxic gold rush, is now reportedly responsible for 2,132 earthquakes in Oklahoma in 2015. The dumping of wastewater under ground is not new and money (**god/notes**) will be made regardless of the price. The ones responsible will be long gone when it is over and the illusion of value, long spent. The price for this disaster will be paid for by the rest of us in the future of death, as we all must learn to drink and breathe toxins. *Once more tombstones will be the legacy of the almighty **god/note** and the deceivers, all under the watchful eyes of the religious.*

As we pump the last of the water out of our precious aquifers, these earthquakes make new cracks in the earth and the pressurize black oozy wastewater (consisting of who knows what, because they don't have to tell us,,, by law,,, brought to us by the Poli-Christians) will mix with the last of the good water supply,,, rendering it 100% useless. *Oklahoma is looking like a good place to be from,,, a long way from as we all slip closer to the inevitable fall off the cliff.*

Man's existence forced over cliff

However, if you think you are safe in your state or your country, think again. It is reported by the EPA (the ones that polluted the Colorado River in the year 2015) that less than 1% of usable surface aquifers are contaminated by industrial landfills. That does not include public landfills. And what is their definition of polluted,,, water that burns? It took the governor of Michigan to warn the people of Flint that they had a problem,,, not the EPA. *I guess they were busy digging up gold mines. Maybe the initials, E.P.A. should stand for, Ever Polluting America.*

The number of landfills has gone from over 18,000 in the early 80s, to today where there are a total of 1,700 left. All are seeping **black ooze** into the land and water we all need to drink. Putting toxins in the ground,,, out of site,,, is going to be a reoccurring problem for decades or until everyone and everything is dead. ***Nothing any of us do is going to stop what is coming. Survivors will live the short term if they are smart,,, but what of the long term. Do you really want to live a life in a heated up, dead world?***

Fukushima radioactive waste has crossed the globe and Japan still has no control over it,,, ***and this is but one meltdown***. They continually store what water they can collect into leaking iron tubs, bolted together. This runoff is caught behind a temporary dam and when it rains all the leaking untapped radioactive runoff is dumped into the sea... again. This government only pretends to control it, like America does with its out of sight out of mind, fracking, waste pumping into the ground.

The **radioactive waste** produced by American corporations is held in **on-site containers**. That means that they, (the government and the power industry) have no clue what to do or how to do it. That means when **god/notes** and government's crash and politicians or any form of government are gone, as well as the power companies (45 year life span tops), the radioactive waste will be left to the winds and drain into the earth and our drinking water and then into the ever rising sea - just like Fukushima. The Japanese don't have the money to contain one of these plants,,, when they all reach the end of their life cycle 30 to 40 years,,, (that they are well into) who is going to pay to clean this all up? When the global **god/notes** crash, there will be no money to clean them all up. *It is in the very near future,,, so where will man go to be safe and live on?* **Radiation is the next long term disaster just on our door steps. This is no less than 10 years away, awaiting the crash of the global god/notes.** *2023-2028*

This should not be news for governments across the globe, because they have been dumping or disposing of radioactive waste in the sea from its conception,,, about 1946. **Across the globe!!!**

There is a report out there that states that 59 U.S. military bases are suffering from **significant water and soil contamination**. I would think that the **FEMA Death Camps** would be part of the 59, because of their age and how the Deceivers within the federal government runs/cover up things, when there is no accountability. *Out of sight, out of mind, bury it in the back yard and let the next guy clean it up safely, concealed under the Secrecy Act. It's the American way,,, it is the religious way,,, it is man's way. Like they keep saying,,, 'America, founded on good Christian principles'. It would seem to be at the core of all mankind,,, deception.*

Forest Fire Chemicals

This is but one more example of the ignorance of man and the pursuit of the almighty god/note.

There is a trade-off going on under our noses, particularly in the western part of the United States, over the use of **chemical retardants** dumped from the air to slow or stop forest fires. The **chemicals** being dumped are allegedly killing fish, ending up in the **streams**, **lakes** and deep in the **aquifers**. Because they are doing their job (suppressing fires… enriching the corporations) every time the wind blows, the air becomes full of these **toxic chemicals** and end up in our lungs. We **breathe,** drink, and eat these **chemicals,** and as we all know, these manmade **chemicals** cause **cancer**.

Because we know forest fires are breaking the bank of most states that are in the way,,, at a point we are going to understand that we just can't pay to fight them anymore. People choose to live in regions of the country that are prone to these outbreaks and their homes are at risk. So make them out of steel that will not burn. Why should the rest of us pay for their lifestyle?

As the water disappears from the land, there will be more fires that will work their way around the globe, making this part of the world a desert once more. Trees that have stood for over 3,000 years will die from lack of water. There are plans to erect water sprinklers to save the forests and keep them green (2016). The plan is to pump good water out of the ground and spray it on these trees; that in a few years there will be no more water to spray and the trees will be dead anyway. ***Can people really be this stupid? YES!!! We need to save the water!!!***

We are... in our ignorance... creating a moonscape of this earth; but to poison the landscape, poison the air and poison the last of the water in the hopes of saving us from what is going to happen anyway, is mind numbingly ignorant. The outcome will be the same,,, no water, no air and people on the move coming after your home, your food and your water. They will kill you for it. ***The killing fields will cross the land, before it is all over and in a few thousand years (maybe) the earth can start to heal from man and all the radiation covering the globe.***

Western Wildfire Increase

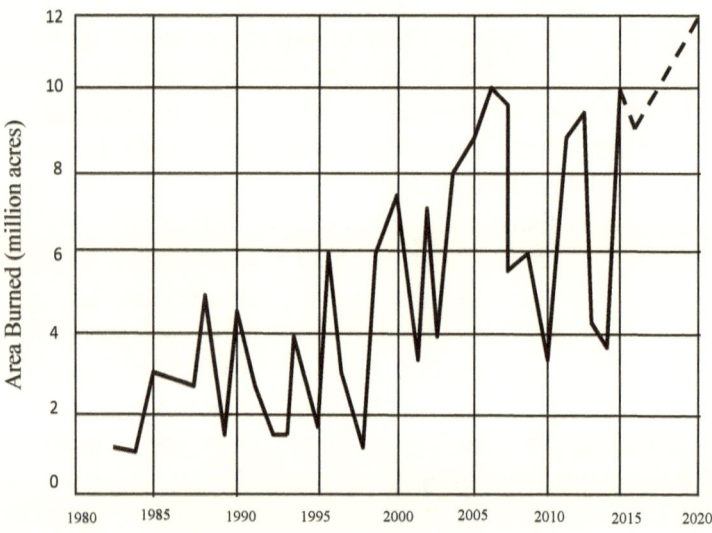

Oceanic Garbage

There is just no end to the destruction of man.

We are entering the land of the unknown as the world has never seen these coming effects ahead of us, which is to be called **The 6th Die Off**. We the **Plastic People**, discard our unwanted debris, mostly plastic in bags made of plastic. An alarming amount of this unwanted plastic ends up in the oceans of the world because people just don't care, or just don't understand. It's that out of sight out of mind thing.

The oceans should not be used for dumping plastic, which takes a very long time to decay and some estimates say it takes up to 500 years before it is completely absorbed back into the land as relatively harmless. Until such time, these plastic bits float in the water and follow the currents to their center.

These circulating currents are called **Gyre** and, to my understanding, there are **5 in the world's oceans today**. To some they are called the **trash vortex** and are growing at an alarming rate. These patches are concentrations of pelagic plastics, chemical sludge and other debris that have been trapped by these oceanic currents.

These are vast stretches of water and some parts have four parts per cubic meter. So in less than 100 years we have gone from clean water full of fish and no pollution, too much death and four parts per meter.

Plastic Beach in Hawaii

Kamilo Beach is also known as the **Plastic Beach**, because everyday <u>tons</u> of plastic debris washes up on this shore. In some estimates the piles of plastic parts are over <u>five feet thick</u>.

The community surrounding the beach tried to clean it up, but there seems to be little point, for the next day more and more trash will just wash up on shore. We earthlings will just have to forget the good times when the beach was pure and pristine and accept other people's trash as the new normal. **But the planet has bigger more pressing problems.**

We see trash littering the streets of third world countries but not so much in America. As these people migrate they bring with them their filthy habits of discarding trash,,, from their hands to the ground. It is someone else's problem now. Only thing is, we who know better, we who know pollution produce disease; we will just have to get used to it. Filth and pollutions would just seem to be part of being a human being. Something inside us says it's okay to do this. I just don't understand and never will.

The utter disregard for those that follow us, is an inherent disorder found in humans, and hear at our end, there will be few places left undamaged by man. Four generations from now, the surviving people, the ones to see it coming will move forward in time, but not without changes.

Rare Earth Elements

The bomb, jet, cell phone and chemical element manufacturers, and all the gadget people, need rare earth elements, at any price. It is a very messy process to produce them. The United States has somehow made environmental laws to protect us the American's and the water; therefore, production has all but stopped in America due to these environmental costs.

However, in China it's another story. This country wants money at any price and has become the leading manufacturer of these Rare Earth Elements. So, the pollution of their land and water is of biblical proportions. The price those people pay is coming at them very hard and very fast.

But the question facing us all is, if we as a people are inherently filthy and there are so many of us now, where can we possibly go when we have completely polluted all the land water and air? If one race of people have taken good care of their land, water and air,,, the ones that did not will just take it. For their need is greater than yours, and for most of these people, they have God and religion on their side. *History has repeatedly shown us (still does) that it is ok to kill and steal as long as you have god on your side.*

Sea Gypsies

I have always looked upon the lifestyle of Sea Gypsies with much envy. They <u>had</u> no port of call and live on the sea in their handmade boats. Some are upwards of 30 feet in length and made without a screw or nail. *A skill about to be lost for good as these people's lifestyle is coming to an end as a wave of destructive humanity engulfs them.*

For the most part, they had the islands to themselves, but not today. The influx of people all wanting to live on the shores has taken over their natural home. The islands once free for them now belong to the rich and they, like the American Indian, the indigenes people are kicked off. The ruling government has permitted them a small stretch of beach for themselves (like the American Indian reservations) and the hotels are fast encroaching, wanting even that small strip of land.

This small group of people is seeing an end to their nomadic lifestyle as the world closes in. There are no more islands, there are no more beaches and the masses are coming with their filth taking the last of the fish as the water heats up.

It is estimated that in thirty years, 70% of the world's population will live on the sea shores. *I am not sure; is this government report of the people moving to the beaches... or the beaches moving to the people?* For these people I fear their removal is coming very soon, for the reefs that they live off of are dying. Global warming, carbon dioxide, and acid rain are killing off the reefs and the fish that live there, as well as their food.

We are seeing our future in them. For the Sea Gypsies, their end is now, not ten years from now.

Great Barrier Reef

This is some of the most disturbing evidence of the truth of Global Warming before us. It reveals the truth that our time is very short indeed, before the sixth die off unfolds.

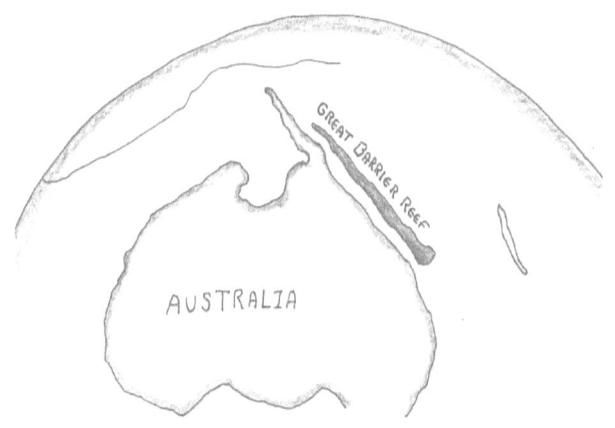

This should be very disturbing to any one of you that can read and comprehend what you are reading. **The Great Barrier Reef** is found off the northeastern part of Australia and is protected by their government (as it should be).

As of 1985, this reef was the largest living group of organisms in the world and can be seen from space. Now, in spite of the value of such a vast living group of coral, it is also home for fish, mollusks, starfish, turtles, dolphins and sharks.

It is one of the last places on the earth that you can still swim with BIG fish that once roamed the seas freely helping to feed the massive growth of man.

It is reported that the big fishing boats of the rich countries have stripped to the ocean floors, over 95% of the fish and other sea life. It is gone.

What will man eat when the last fish is removed and eaten? *Maybe the rich will tell us what the English said to the occupied Irish during the potato famine 1845 to 1852, "Let them eat grass... and they did"*

The sad part of this is that since 1985 50% of this reef has disappeared from the earth. Now that is just 30 years and half is gone for good and do you think this is going to stop? What caused the reef to disappear is carbon dioxide, put in the air by man and now it is acid in the (continuing to heat up) ocean waters, killing the reefs around the world.

The effects of this acid are growing, not decreasing and that means with the acid in the water now, the **Great Barrier Reef** will be gone in 15 years or less. *My estimate is it will be gone in 5 to 7 years because of the water heating up.*

The chart below shows just how fast it will happen based on history and our lack of will to face the facts that man's pumping fossil fuels into the air and water is a devastating thing.

Decline in percentage of reef surface covered by live coral across the Great Barrier Reef, Australia, 1985-2030.

2017 60% gone

The Great Barrier Reef will be only a memory in our short future as the waters get hotter and more polluted and sink out of site in the upcoming flooding. I put its end at around 2024 and 2026.

Nature's Rights

Chapter Seven

God
And
Starvation

Christians killing non-Christians and Atheists

The above image is from the book Jesus Christ in Canaan. A detailed look at the Christian religion and how it affects world conflict up to this very day. The crusades are with us and doing just fine,,, killing the Muslim's all across the world.

Today as I write these words in 2015, 10% of the world's population (7.4 Billion People) is <u>hungry</u> and that number is growing. For those of you that cannot do the math that is 7.2 million people, every day in these,,, the last of the abundant times.

The world is becoming a very small place these days as there just seems to be more and more people everywhere. So many mouths to feed and all of them want the latest gadget to add to the waste pile of life. Seemingly, technology and vanity are hand in hand,,, pushing us all faster and faster to the brink of the **6th die off** that is ahead of us all.

The landfills across the globe are full of such waste from the Gadget people and these cancer chemicals of death are seeping into our drinking water all across the globe. Endless wars, that fill the needs of the very few, to accumulate more **god/notes** by getting oil, selling war supplies and reconstruction material, and of course, killing the wrong god people, seem to be the goals of these gods these days. *For someone on the outside it* *starts to look like all religions pray to a god with horns and a pointy tail,,, do you smell sulfur?*

These power wars are causing an epic migrant crisis in Europe (2016,2017), as those unwilling to fight and die for their land, their principles, their religions and yes, their gods,,, run to safer places with their mouths open and their righteous hands out, begging,,, demanding. Those that take care of their government, their water, their food and their resources,,, must now care for the new starving masses,,, that did not take care of their government, their food or their resources, and I will add,,, will not, for it is up to God to do that. *As I predicted in Global Financial Super Heating,,, it is starting.*

As of 2016, Turkey has taken an estimated two million people into their small country of just over 70 million people. These masses of people are running from Syria's war that looks as though it was all over the gods. This care and feeding of the displaced is a growing business and much money is being made feeding the newly starving. They are held in government camps to prevent them from mixing with the population as they are in another country that doesn't want them either.

1960s and 70s

Germany took in so many migrant workers that its citizens were displaced from their jobs and homes. You see, these desperate homeless migrants will do anything and for less money. Who benefits, who would want cheap labor? Big business,,, while the rest pay for cheap labor with welfare. There were riots in the streets of Germany, a war of religion and cultures for cheap labor.

Today, all across Europe tens of thousands of citizens are protesting the browning of their countries. The Islamization of their once white Christian country is too much to endure and out into the street they march in protest. The new guests in these countries also are protesting, showing the world their anger over their treatment as <u>guests</u> in a foreign land. Just what is it they want that the Germans are fearful of? Food, water, jobs, their homes and to enforce their barbaric dark ages religion on the people of Germany is all. *Just look at how they behave when they are not given what they want. Just look at the roads where they walked to come to Germany. The filth is piled a foot deep. Who can blame the Germans for not wanting this present day turmoil of cultures? Remember they have lived through this before.*

April 6, 2015

This movement is all over the world and anti-Islam rallies have brought out tens of thousands, from fear of the Muslim community. The **'Reclaim Australia'** is but one more example as race color and most dangerous of all,,, religion and God,,, divide us all from each other. The Australian immigration detention facilities are across the country and on the territory of Christmas Island. A Christian named island is holding Muslims away from the populous. The fear is,,, and some think wise thinking,,, *when there is no food or water, who will be the first to go? The ones that*

181

have the wrong god and the wrong skin color will be the first. Australia is saying,,, "We don't want them either!"

German and England White Movements

The wars that are spilling over borders bringing unwanted cultures and unwanted gods to once peaceful lands face all the people of Europe today. **'Britain First'** (reportedly) is a political party against mass immigration or the Islamization of their country. (Wrong god, wrong skin)

The UN estimates 31,000 refugees have fled to Italy so far this year as of 04/16/15, with 900 estimated to have died in the journey. Profiteers peddling a better life in Europe, sell standing room only on ships heading north. It is rumored that the tiny country of Malta has run out of room to bury the unwelcome dead coming to their small island.

News accounts of the migrants dead at sea because of boats capsizing seem to be every day, but you only need to look to the south of this poverty and war torn region to see more. Death in South Africa greets the same immigrants as they to, the south, don't want them either. The thinking is, resources are thin, (money, food) and should they not be spent on their own people,,, instead of foreigners. After all, it is their money; they saved it for their people. Not foreigners with the wrong skin color and wrong god. Death awaits the immigrants at home and in new lands that don't want them.

Many believe they should have stayed and fought the wars as the people of Europe did in their land. As most people have done before,,, (like the American Indians did) defending their land, their country from the religious invaders.

What are they running from, war, poverty, starvation or is it the wrong god people? I don't believe it is at all what we are being told and to better understand we have to go back in time.

Many believe they are running from the Christians, in another long and ongoing Christian crusade, where the Christians are killing the Muslims because they have the wrong god. Look closely by some accounts, Christians are reportedly killing 95% of all Muslims killed in the world today. If you're Christian,,, that is a number for your gods to be proud of. To understand why America is over there killing, creating destabilization in that region, read Jesus Christ in Canaan.

October 17, 2015

In the German town of Riesa, it is now being reported that the far right is growing in support. The NPD National Democratic Party does not want to pay the price to feed these asylum seekers. They don't want to become the world's social welfare office as America has. *They can see the end of their resources and the Germans want their stored resources spent on their people, not immigrants and certainly not Muslims. This rising up of anger is growing across the world, as many prepare for Armageddon.*

God and Papal Supremacy

The faithful of this religion have been with us for a very long time and it would seem their goal is to **force** their gods onto each one of us. **(For more information, read my book** ˌ*Scrupulosity***)** Religion, it would seem, has more to do with money, sex, control and lavish life styles, than about saving souls to live together with the old man in the big spaceship in the sky. It would seem that there is to be but one god for us all and his followers are willing to kill anyone that gets in the way. *The righteous have self anointed rights to kill and seize property, including oil and most important,,, water and food. They have been doing this for thousands of years. This is not new. The rest of the world just sits back and say and do nothing, in fear of reprisals.*

Christians and Catharism

From the concept of Christianity, this religion has had many differing views as to what this religion should be.

In the 12th to the 14th centuries, the followers of Jesus Christ, in Europe, were split in half. The Pope could not control the half called Catharism. So as the story goes; the pope declared war on followers of Catharism and offered to anyone that would "take up arms" and kill them, the land and all property belonging to the concord followers of the wrong branch of Christianity. *What happened to that, "Thou shalt not kill" thing?*

Both sides believed in the same gods (making it one religion, Christianity) and yet the subtle differences set one loving peaceful side to kill the other and what a prize offered. I can claim to be a Christian, and with the Popes permission and blessing, go into my neighbor's home and kill him and then take his land and suffer no reprisals. Not ever from the gods. "The spoils of war."

You see, the Christians have a long line of murder, war and stealing to enrich themselves and that mentality lives on to this very day. Only most people worry so much about the next life that they give little thought to this life. Giving themselves the right to, rape a child, seize another's property (spoils of war) and commit genocide in their god's name. **What god(s) would want this?**

Today, looking back at the history of Christianity, one finds many Christian crusades where they have committed genocide; annihilating whole cultures and civilizations for their gods. It would seem hacking them to death and stealing their land, their silver, their gold, is part of god's plan on all sides. This is in their history, their present and I know it is in their future. **See chapter 8, FEMA Death Camps.**

The good people within the Roman Catholic Church have a doctrine called **Papal Supremacy**. This doctrine empowers one person,,, the Pope,,, **by reason of his office as vicar of Christ,,, full and supreme UNIVERSAL power over the whole**

church. The Pope also enjoys **supreme full and universal power in the care of souls**. *Isn't that nice? I wonder if that includes the ones he murders in his genocides?*

So it is easy to see how these people with their self appointed grandeur and self imposed **supreme power over all**, would want to destroy anything and any one that got in their way. (i.e.) *wrong gods, wrong skin and worst sin of all,,, wrong religion (Mormon, Presbyterian, Jehovah), all must die under the Popes supreme power.* ***This is what the future holds,,, the right religion or the righteous will eat and the wrong religion or less righteous will starve or be eaten.***

Were we supposed to wait until he was

dead?

Whoever feeds on my flesh and drinks my blood has eternal life, and I will raise him up on the last day.

William J. Ryan copyright © 2014 #08

Jewish Deicide

The Jews (those with perfect souls) killed their man god (Christ, also known as The King of Jews) and therefore, the Christians now have in their arsenal of righteousness, a weapon called **Jewish Deicide**. It was the Christian led countries that divided up the Middle East, (drawing new maps) creating new countries, arming those that would sell oil to kill those that would not sell oil and giving **Arab stolen land** to the Jews. *(To learn more, read my book Jesus Christ in Canaan)*

And people wonder why the Muslims want to kill all the people in the west (Christians).

This infuriated the Muslim people (as it would anyone) and they are still trying to straighten out what the Christians did just 100 years ago, when the maps were drawn. For someone on the outside, it looks like this was done deliberately, to set up the Jews for the slaughter by the Muslims. Divide and conquer, the Christian plan, (we don't want the Jews in our country so send them to the holy land to fight, guard it and die, for the Christians) is going to backfire against the Jews,,, part of the plan of **Jewish Decide**. The Pope must be very proud of his work of death on the earth as he stands next to one of his gods.

This religion is the one I would support if I were a weapon manufacturer and wanted more **god/notes**. (However like all manufactures I would sell to both sides.) These Christian people of the only god to be,,, are willing to kill and that is what those, who sell war supplies want as customers. It makes it nice for them that they don't let that **'Thou shall not kill'** thing get in the way.

It would seem to be **the new meaning of God,,, KILL**. *Now maybe I am not so bright,, does this god have hooves and a pointy tail and horns? It would make more sense then.* **Over the next four generations, regardless of the gods, who will eat and who will drink will be the ones on top of humanities enormous death pile.**

But then there is the part where **the Pope enjoys universal power in the care of all SOULS.** I am just not sure whose souls the good Christians are empowered to care for. Well, we know it is not Muslims souls,,, Christians do love to kill them. It's not the Jews souls, Christians also love to kill them as well. How about their own soles,,, other good Christians? Well we know they love their Christian pedophiles (because the pope hides them from prosecution) and do all they can to protect them,,, there is some strange love there I will never understand.

But what of the little ones that are force to come to the church for guidance, (some call that brain washing) and get raped by the priest of the Christian gods? It would appear these (souls) victims of rape are cast aside like so much trash,,, and yet, they are Christians too,,, or were.

Then there are the crusades against themselves such as the 1300s and Christian vs. Catholicism. So many dead over god and these killed over the same gods. *I just will never get religion and the stupid people that give their power over themselves to it,,,* **Scrupulosity**.

Food and Weed Control

The weed control people (chemical manufactures) that love to make or turn, toxins into dollars or **god/notes**, without a care for the land and water or the cancer it creates in people,,, as well as the starvation that is to follow,,, have been doing just fine. They are raking in their trillions, but look at the mess that is left (like oil and nuclear power). It is like the (fracking) gas companies when they are done making their trillions of **god/notes**,,, the mess to the environment (air, land and water) is someone else's problem, because they will be gone,,, rich and gone. **But all their numbers on a spread sheet (money in banks) will not save them from the 6th die off that is coming that they helped create.**

*This is part of the free market system. They are free to destroy the land, air, water, sea and people, as long as they are able to make or take as many **god/notes** as they can. From where I am sitting, no one will stop them, but Mother Nature utilizing **Nature's Rights** and her gift of death.*

It is believed by many that the toxins sprayed on farm fields are killing the bees that pollinate (grow food) the plants. The bee die off is ever growing each year. **No bees means, no fresh food as new strains on existing food are placed on what is left to eat**.

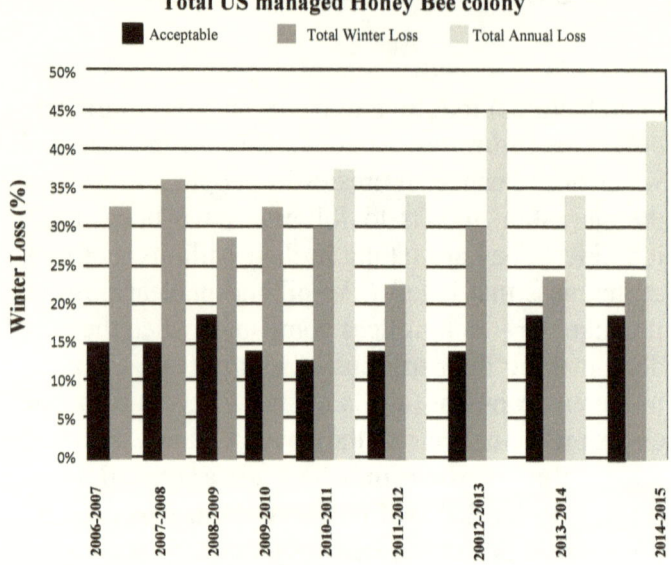

Total US managed Honey Bee colony

■ Acceptable ▪ Total Winter Loss ▪ Total Annual Loss

The honey bee population has been declining for years, with the U.S. losing nearly half of its hives yearly. In the 1970s, our honey bee colonies were at 4 million, now they are at 2.5 million.

A study was conducted by the Bee Informed Partnership in collaboration with the Apiary Inspectors of America and the U.S.D.A. The preliminary results indicated that beekeepers in the U.S. were the hardest hit in the summer of 2014, with an average loss of 27.4% of their hives, compared to the 19.8% the previous summer.

While winter numbers improved slightly at about 0.6% less than the previous winter, the honey bee death rise is still too high for long-term survival. Colony losses were 23.1% for the 2014-

15 winter months, which is normally the higher loss period.

October 15, 2015

It was reported that The United States Department of Agriculture announced there is an **increase of herbicide resistant weeds** in the U.S. agricultural system,,, (businesses that grow food for money or **god/notes**).

*Now let me see if I understand this problem. In an effort to eliminate jobs in America, the farming industry has (the ones that put the small farmer out of business in the 1970's),,, without a care for the land, water or the people,,, pursued the almighty **god/note** and it is not working out very well. The weeds are doing just fine (via Mother Nature) and returning with a vengeance. Only now the land and water are poisoned,,, oh yeah,,, and the people, livestock and small creatures are also poisioned. So it is not a good idea to dump toxins on the land and in the water, where it will remain for decades to exchange short lived profits for long range devastation. And what is the damage to the people that trust governments to regulate them?*

Only our children and grandchildren will pay that price. The next four generations from now will see and know of such horrendous death. The land will be barren of life and they will know the taste of human flesh.

The United States Department of Agriculture or U.S.D.A's Natural Resource Conservation Service or the N.R.C.S is offering money in the form of financial assistance under its

Environmental Quality Incentives Program or the E.Q.I.P. for herbicide resistant weed control.

So in the past 60 years pouring toxins on the ground has not worked out so well and now the government, bought and paid for by the rich, has welfare money for the corporations that bought up all the farms in the 70s via the government's grain payment seizure.

The U.S.D.A.'s Animal and Plant Health Inspections Service or the A.P.H.I.S, will promote use of **genetically engineered** (GE) crops. *Now who knows what type of toxins or cancer is in these new plants for us all to eat. You can bet your ass they are not going to tell you the truth.*

The U.S.D.A. is partnering with the Weed Science Society of America or the W.S.S.A, *(now I did not make up those names)* and is providing funds to develop education and outreach materials regarding herbicide resistant weeds. *Now that will fix it. This is starting to remind me of an old poorly written poorly directed black and white 'B' rated monster movie made back in the 1930's.*

We all can see the ending before it starts and we know how it is going to turn out,,, death. When you try to kill (weeds) Nature's Rights have a strange way of coming back at you,,, tenfold.

The problem is real. This government can make up all the silly names it wants. The politicians provide welfare for the rich so big business can create all the new poisons it can to dump on the ground and into the water we drink, without a care. They end up poisoning the land and water, nothing is going to head off what is coming,,,

NOTHING!!! For the short term, we are moving backwards in time. To a day when only the rich had food and the rest of us starved or ate grass or our young. Human life is about to become very, very, very cheap.

I am not talking of 100 years or of 50 years but 5 to 10 years tops. I have tried to show you that it is all aspects of life, food, water and most important,,, the air we breathe. The 6th die off is standing at our door step.

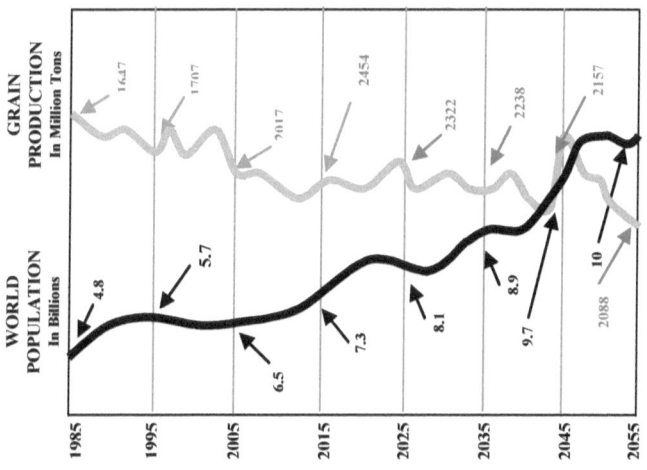

Our world population is growing at 1.7 percent each year. It is said that by 2050, the world population will reach up to 10 billion. This chart shows what happens when population increases and food production decreases. Grain production has fallen 8 percent since 1981. It has dropped below 1.4 percent per year since 1991. If our grain production keeps dwindling, we will not have enough food to feed everyone in the world very soon.

This is the face of our future. The rich will eat and the poor will starve and eat their young. Governments cannot incarcerate them all so the need to have **(FIMA) death camps** is real. We all should know the selection will be based upon the gods and the color of your skin.

Horse Meat for Human Consumption

The following just makes me sick to the core, as I see the growing end of the American way of life and our society being pulled back down to its animal core and roots; much like the rest of the world and our new American third world future (people that don't know what toilet paper is). It was such a short ride of decency and morality lasting only from WWII until the 70s. About the time we dumped gold and all morality for the almighty **god/note**.

August 10, 2009

Pet quarter horse in Miami Florida,,, killed and slaughtered for its meat. Who would do such a thing and why? Are we that hungry in America? Or are they selling this poor animal meat to some shop, some store, or some fast food outlet? *They just could not have been Americans brought up with* *any values,,, unless it is the values of corporate America.* **This is the future,,, get use to it.**

June 29, 2013

It is being reported that the USDA, the **United States Department of Agriculture** (that is us in America) has approved **horse** slaughterhouses to produce meat for **human consumption**. Yes, that is right,,, I said horse meat for people to eat,,, and where have you been eating your horse meat? This is a new low indeed,,, but where will it stop? *It will stop at the end of all life,,, all living things,,, then turn back upon ourselves in the form of cannibalism. God has in the past accepted this (eat my flesh,,, drink by blood) and god will in the future, accepting this as we consume each other to live on into the short future we have left as things heat up.*

What more needs to be said? Horse meat for humans has been illegal in the United States because it carries phenylbutazone that would put you at risk of illness and or death. *(Horse meat was banned for consumption in 2007, when the USDA decided not to inspect horse slaughter houses, but in 2013, Obama revisited the issue and lifted the ban (I am sure for some type of consumption). It is claimed that horse meat is more nutritious and lean than beef. YUCK! It is said that the reason we don't eat horse meat is due to religion.)* But per this report phenylbutazone a **small risk**. *It's a small risk for only the ones that eat red meat. And have any of you seen commercials announcing this new additive to your fast food burgers? I don't* *think so, but they make more money buying this dangerous cheaper meat for you suckers to eat. I can find no requirements of these food restaurants to tell you the food you are about to eat is,,, or was a **horse**. This is undoubtedly the best recommendation for becoming a vegetarian I have seen yet. **So much is changing so fast and without our knowledge and our being aware of the full ramifications. Governments do not care,,, religions do not care,,, it is up to you to care.***

March 13, 2015

Thousands of animals rescued from illegal slaughter house in Miami-Dade area. A large third world community,,, with third world values. Reportedly, some 3000 animals were kept in unsanitary conditions, starved and killed in inhumane methods. *Now that image has to make that burger taste a lot better. I am starting to see a scene from Texas Chain Saw Massacre. Will these meat supply warehouses buy red meat from anyone? Yes. If that is true,,, and it is,,, who is to say it is horse? Maybe it is chopped up dogs or cats and yes even people,,, Clearly no one is looking, including you who eat this meat you once thought was cow. **It will just keep getting worse.***

July 23, 2015

On this day a slaughtered quarter horse was found in Hialeah Florida. The joy of having a horse in one's life in America is coming to an end; because some view these animals as only **god/notes** for the taking, their lives ending in a sad and brutal fashion,,, for their meat. *Is this to become the new* *normal? Will the police find human trunks in the ditches? Their arms and legs chopped off and sold to the highest bidder. Then it's served up to you with dipping sauce.*

October 15, 2015

An expensive prized show horse was found killed and slaughtered on a farm in Palmetto Florida.

*As a pet lover, I can't imagine what it would be like to find someone you loved, cared for, fed every day, talked to and took for walks, was hacked to bits in your yard, for **god/notes**. I would be tempted to spend every cent I had to hunt down these butchers and kill them myself; by slaughtering them and then eating their flesh at a barbecue. I would find them and they would know the price,,, my price,,, street justice. **Our future.***

Is this what happens when you let third world people, of no moral background, mix and come into this country? Someone had to buy this meat or was it meant for a family and they can't find a job so this is how they put meat on their table? Your pet,,, and without a care.

*Another disturbing part of all of this is, now that the United States Department of Agriculture has approved horse meat for people to eat,,, where is it? Who is serving this,,, once a pet,,, to you the red meat eaters of America? Most likely they are serving it at a fast food giant near you or your local supermarket. They only care about the almighty **god/notes**.*

The question to keep in mind as we slip down this slope back to the dark ages is... At what point will the USDA approve human meat for human consumption? Will they call it Soy lent Green?

Water Is Food

September 21, 2015

Man's quest to fill the empty belly of man has no bounds. Every country is clearing its wasted land (not productive, not making money),,, forest,,, and planting food,,, growing **god/notes**. Down on the lower half of the world they are seeing a weather change that has allegedly ended their rain and stopped them from growing food all together. The country is Indonesia and their crop failure is blamed on El Nino (Jesus Christ).

At the same time Indonesia is pursuing the almighty **god/note** and clearing their old growth forest (via burning it,,, consuming air) to feed this ever growing hungry world (and growing more hungry every day). They are burning everything in sight. Reportedly, the forest and peat moss is now smoldering and causing heavy thick smoke choking people for hundreds of miles.

It would seem that the blame is being placed on a few farmers that were clearing their land and set a blaze to the country side,,, with dreams of making more money,,, **god/notes**. But it is a fact that the deforestation of Indonesia has been going on for the past 100 years,,, much like the rest of the world. In the 1900s, Indonesia had an estimated 85% of its country as **rain** forest.

*Now stop and look at the words **rain forest** and what does it mean? The words mean,,, rain forest,,, a forest that produces rain because of its trees. A cycle of life that works, using the balance of **Nature's Rights** to life. When you cut down all the trees, (kill) you cut down the chances of this land doing anything but becoming a desert.*

Look to the sky's for more hot spots to break through and cause super heating. When we consume or convert all the air the sun can and will come through and cause record highs and death.

In the next ten years (2025 to 2026), it is estimated that the remaining forest and all its inhabitants will be gone. These estimates did not include burning it and no rain for two years. **Death and migration** is their future (Indonesia) as the state (government) now feeds the farmers.

Due to the loss of air, storms that are created when water vapor builds up, cannot happen because there is no place for the storms to build. The water vapor needs air to become a storm and make rain. No air,,, no rain.

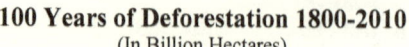

100 Years of Deforestation 1800-2010
(In Billion Hectares)

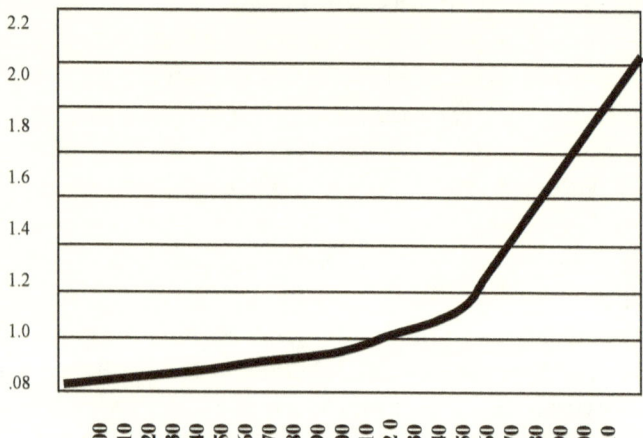

Aquifers across the world are disappearing before our eyes and the following chart show how quickly the Ogallala Aquifer is disappearing. This aquifer is under 7 states and shrinking fast. We are talking about a time span of just about 50 years.

Farming, gas fracking and nuclear power harvesting, has all but destroyed this aquifer and by my estimates water from this region will be useless and the masses will migrate to a town near you to take your water, kill your pets, eat your food and live in your home.

Time line of drying up or toxic Ogallala Aquifer is 2023 to 2028.

Chart showing the Ogallala Aquifer shrinking.

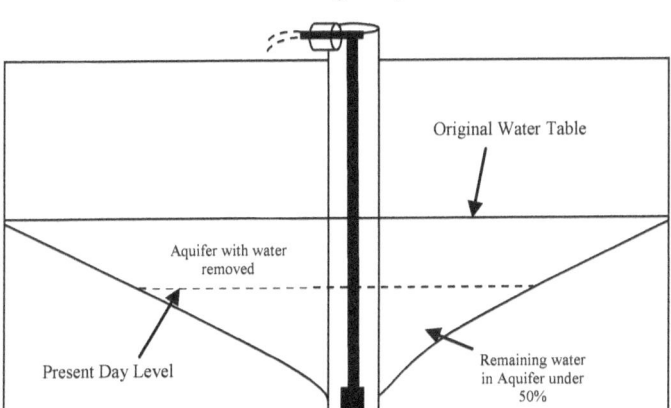

March 21, 2015

Sinkholes are forming each year around the Dead Sea as they have taken out the drinking water from the ground. Their future is ours as their government has mismanaged their resources as has ours. This is Mother Nature's Revenge. The balance of all things must be observed, for without balance there is nothing. This is her lesson to us all, unfortunately it is too late, for the 6th die off is upon u. It will begin in, but a decade or less away.

Aquifers Other Purpose
Now this is important, for as life moves forward this will affect all of us most dramatically.

It makes me sick to think that over the past 10,000 years, (or longer) rain water and snow melt have accumulated under the earth for just the rich to exploit and turn into **god/notes**. But could there be another purpose to aquifers that has affected and protected all of us without our knowing it? Could these precious concealed, underground lakes, be doing something we can't yet see, hear or smell besides hold up the land?

These aquifers across the globe play one more vital role in life here on earth and that is in **cooling** the ground deep beneath our feet. Deep under the ground these pools of water are keeping the magma from bursting through the surface. Like a lid on a pressure cooker or insolated gloves, we all need these aquifers right where they are, to keep a lid on what is under them.

Yellowstone National Park is a primary example of just such a situation where the pressure of the immense magma deep in the earth is held in check by the aquifers cooling water. What makes this park so beautiful are all the HOT springs, bubbling mud beds and old faithful the geyser.

The following two drawings show what I believe is going on under the surface and how we are being protected by these natural cooling aquifers. Remove them for **god/notes** and only one thing can happen.

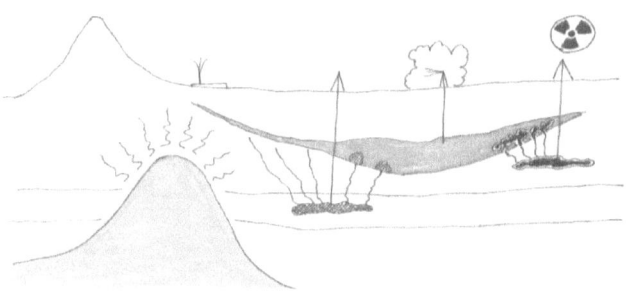

Cut-away view of the Ogallala Aquifer and the cooling effect it has on the enter core of the planet protecting us from its devastation.

Location of the Ogallala Aquifer and its shrinking over the past 50 years and the next 30 years.

Nature's Rights

Chapter Eight

Martial Law

FEMA
Death Camps

View of what is believed to be one of the 30,000 FEMA Guillotines bought by this government for use in the United States on American citizens.

Nature's Rights

Armageddon: (Latin: Armageddon) 'the site of a gathering of armies for a battle during the end times, the end of the world scenario.'

One Christian interpretation is: *'Jesus (the man god) will return to earth and defeat the Antichrist,,, or the Beast.'* **And here may be the justification or as I call it, Scrupulosity (self-imposed righteousness) of the thousands of years of Christian killing,,, it's for their gods. So that makes it ok? If the innocent suffer at their hands,,, as they do,,, is that not a sin? Something that Lucifer, Satan and the Devil,,, the fallen angel that, like Christ, sat next to god would be ok with?** The Christian dream or belief is that their dead, man Jew god, will return to earth and kill people,,, the ones that believe in the wrong god. Religion is so bazaar and people are so ignorant...

Now stop and think for a moment, children are taught about god at a young age. All innocent children are shown a god and all his magical

power. Are we all not innocent because we are taught to kill for god? There by deserving of forgiveness?

I think he (this son of god) will have a big job, for from where I sit, all churches, mosques, synagogues and temples are full of the **Beast,** wanting only to kill the innocent and other non-religious (followers of their faith), wrong religion or god that have gone astray. If Jesus kills all the ones full of the alleged **Beast,,,** who will be left, for the beast is in them all?

After the collapse of the global **god/notes** and the fall of the global stock markets, food and water will quickly become the number one concern of each person on the planet. It is now becoming that in 2016 as 10% of the world population go hungry every day. Its cost will skyrocket, and when the poor and hungry riot in the street, blindly striking out,,, the police will be called in,,, outnumbered and overwhelmed.

The only thing is, the police are under the watchful eye of the little brother system. That system is you and me, with our home security systems, our phones and our car recorders. Today, most every step they take and/or word they use is recorded via police cams and each time (for the most part), their actions are being questioned, scrutinized and critiqued. They lay their lives on the line every day, and if they should make one mistake, we pounce on them with both feet.

Not a job I would want, because you are hated by the bad guys and by the good people as well as your employer. Because he watches your every move, like you were a thief, or a crook. That is a lot of pressure to be under for a f**ken job. I would rather drive a truck than be a cop! So would most other normal people it seems,.

The only people that would be attracted to this type of work are the mentally disturbed. Those that enjoy brutalizing people, somehow getting some type of sick satisfaction from other people's pain as they use their Legal Power to control them; and if caught,,, their crimes are covered up (like those within the Christian church). That is why the news is full of police brutality, for who would want these jobs? Only the mentally disturbed that takes pleasure in inflicting pain on others. Like priest pedophiles are drawn to the catholic church,,, what better place to hide,,, then in plain sight.

Because normal people (not mentally disturbed) could not brutalize people in this way, the good ones of us are not drawn to this line of work. Recently, it was reported that the police departments are scrambling to fill open positions within their ranks. Some departments report they are down 90% in applicants from just 10 years ago. Is it the low pay or do they see the future and just not want to be on the wrong side of the collapse? Or would they rather be home with their families when things unfold?

The question is, how will it start? Will it begin as the riot of Camden, New Jersey did in 1969? Or will it start from the day the government turns on its unarmed people and guns them down in the street, as they did in the Kent State shooting on May 4, 1970? The inevitable is coming, but it is still not clear when exactly it will happen, but look to the collapse of the dollar (**god/notes**) and the inability the illusion of "we the people," to govern ourselves. That will bring the never ending **Martial Law** that is on our doorstep, as the thirsty and starving are turning up everywhere.

Venezuela is one recent example of the future of America and the rest of the world as their dollar collapses in 2016 and the government cannot feed its people. They are starving and now stealing food to feed their families. We are on the precipice of the dark ages as we enter the 6th die off.

* * * * * * * *

News reports from the slow decay of the United States as the future unfolds.

December 5, 2013

Due to budget cuts across this country after the crash of 2008, the police departments are getting fewer qualified recruits to fill the ranks of guardians of the current laws. Fewer people are applying and more are being disqualified from consideration, creating new and growing shortages.

June 10, 2015

Police departments across the country are facing a shortage of new recruits. This shortage of applicants in some cities is down more than 90%. Fewer qualified people are trying to join the force and take on one of the most dangerous jobs you can get, next to being a professional government whistleblower.

The tougher standards, low pay, and being hated on all three sides (crooks, God people and superiors), plus being shot at just is not drawing the masses it once did and we are left with the deranged. Not even the masochists that love to brutalize people are coming to apply in the numbers they once did,,, all those rules and all those cameras make it so hard to have fun brutalizing people.

Now because there are shortages of police, the governors of each state will need to call out the National Guard to get the riots under control. When the starving can't be controlled by the police, can't be controlled by the National Guard (because they are overseas fighting a religious oil war,,, killing Muslims) street justice will take over. When the burning of towns and cities begins, the rich will not have things they want or need, and that is when the president will declare **Martial Law**. *Under military Law, the FEMA Relocation camps (**death camps**) will be activated and a new world order will be put into place.* **Those who complain or dare to speak out in defiance (like myself),,, will pay the ultimate price,,, the loss of their heads.**

May 1, 1945

In the town of Demmin Germany, hundreds of people committed suicide after the invasion of the **Soviet Red Army**. Their fear of the atrocities committed by these soldiers pushed them over the edge,,, that and maybe 5 years of war. Death is viewed as better than life under military rule.

January 2, 2015

More and more of the justice system is in the private hands of corporations. (It should be noted, this is outlawed in some countries) These privately held incarceration (jail) corporations make a profit and that becomes their top priority,,, money. They make **god/notes** by filling every bed. There cannot be any early release. Probation equals loss of revenues for their investors. A problem state run facilities don't have. They should want less in prison,,, just not here in America, as it unwinds.

If you think it was easy for the rich to buy justice before,,, it just got a lot easier. Just pay a price and upgrade your room to a suite overlooking the lake and you can have room service. The rich move up and the poor never get out, enriching the rich. *Only in America,,,* no really,,, only in a corrupt America.

December 9, 2014

Reportedly, there is a study of the CIA's detention and interrogation program. It is to some, known as the **"Torture Report."** Allegedly it consists of 6,800 pages. *And you thought I was long winded.* The overall belief by some is, this mostly classified report shows us all that the CIA answers to no man. They truly are above the law. ***You or I could fall anytime, as its next victim. All people are just its prey. The game is on!***

Bill of Attainder
(present day)

Attainder is in English criminal law to mean metaphorical (Christian God) "stain" or "corruption of blood," and those condemned for such a crime face felony or treason charges. Religion in government, doling out God's punishment without justice... A system left over from the dark ages and **still with us today**. Yes that is right,,, as long as we let religion,,, any religion in to our government,,, regardless of the pretense of its good intentions,,, there is always the dark side,,, hence, **Separation of Church and State**, the First Amendment to the Constitution of the united states.

Is the act of a legislature declaring a person or group,,, guilty of some crime and punishing them all,,, without at trial,,, here with us today? The end effect of such a bill is to nullify the targeted person's civil rights. *The innocent have no rights under this Christian God.* The concept of **Bill of Attainder** goes back to Henry the Eighth in 1509, where such power was used to **remove the Roman Catholic blood sucking** power from his land.

Today (and this should make you sick), such laws are found within the United States of America's Federal Government's power over its people; to take their property without a trial. Your car can be seized (stolen from you) as well as your money,,, while you have **not been found guilty in a court**. If you fly on a plane with too much cash,,, it (the cash) can be seized without a trial, regardless of how you got the cash. *As long as no one speaks*

213

*up,,, nothing will happen,,, they get to keep your money. Now, this is with us today and happening all across the land,,, **<u>without a trial</u>**. One person can accuse you of a crime and take your property. **Why no one is challenging this Bill of Attainder is beyond me,,, but it will make no difference in the outcome of the future,,, pounding at our door, unless the Government just takes it all.**

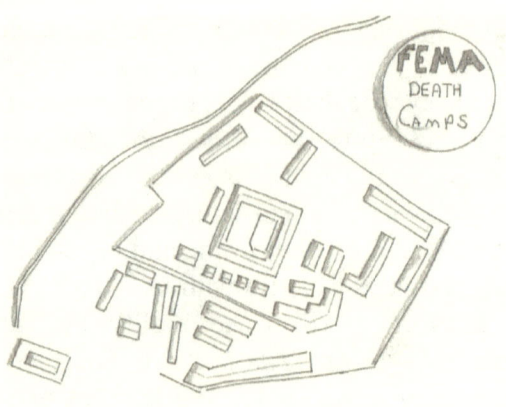

Death Camps

Around 1959, the Kaechon Internment Camp was established in North Korea as a **forced labor camp**, (remember those words,) set up for political prisoners. *I will most likely be one of those modern day political prisoners in their **FIMA Death Camps**.*

This Kaechon Internment camp is still in effect today and controlling its people. The atrocities going on within these camps is still not totally revealed; for their government,,, like America,,, keeps this information classified. *That would be to protect its people from the perceived terrorists within their borders,,, like America,,, as it too is run like an Autocracy Theocracy.*

Many of its prisoners were born under the North Korea's **"Three Generations of Punishment,"** rule. The ones found guilty (with or without a trial) of a crime would be sent to the camps with their entire family. The next two generations would be born there and most likely die there. *I am sure this would include intense brain washing like that found in the Christian church,,, starting at birth.* **How do you ever help those crushed souls? You cannot,,, just as you cannot undo the brainwashing of all religions. Maturity, education, logic and time show us all that there is a path out of its insanities, but it is too late for most. They will go to their graves believing such nonsense.**

Punishment could include having one's finger tips cut off or months of torture until the freedom and peace of death. This is what happens when one unquestioned entity rises to the top,,, **like the CIA**.

Citizens Commission to Investigate the FBI

The bravery of some people is utterly remarkable. This activist group calling themselves

Citizens Commission to Investigate the FBI (today would be classified as a terrorist origination) broke into the offices of the FBI in Media, PA on March 8, 1970. They forwarded stolen documents to newspapers (like today's **WikiLeaks**) all over the country. This handful of brave young people, were responsible for helping to bring an end to the Vietnam War (or an end to war profiteering of big business) at that time and in that religious war. They then slipped underground and were never found,,, until recently,,, as they came forward. *Regardless of your view of their actions,,, these are very brave, common, ordinary people, trying to do the right thing and they did,,, saving countless lives on both sides. Some think we need more people like this today.*

Peace Symbol

The widely known Peace Symbol above reportedly is the semaphore signals for the letters "N" and "D" standing for Nuclear Disarmament. A campaign started in 1958 and this image is now all over the world.

COINTELPRO

These are covert and at times illegal projects conducted by the United States Federal Bureau of Investigation (FBI),,, this American government.

The acronym for the FBIs **CO**unter **INTEL**ligence **PRO**gram; It was created and reportedly took place from 1956 to 1971 and the tactics are still used to this day. The FBI states its motive was "protecting national security." But who's security are they truly protecting? *One more example of just how absolute power will corrupt absolutely.*

The CIA is the one now with unlimited budget and that one listens and stores every word you say (CIA tracking) on your Smart phone. That is the governments chip in your brain. See George Orwell's 1956 film Animal Farm, written in 1948 just after WWII. What he must have seen that made him write those words and come up with such concepts,,, long before we had computers on a massive scale.

Debtors' Prison

Debtors' Prisons were a common way to deal with unpaid debt, in Western Europe (Christian) in the dark days. For the most part unlawful in America until Social Security started to target taxpayers for their **parents' debts** from decades ago. Now, this is not **your debt** but someone else's debt and now you must pay for their **alleged** crimes **against the state,,, and without a trial**. Without due process of law, you will assume the debts of others,,, in the new old Christian America as we march backwards in time.

*Wow! The hands of time are turning back before our eyes, without so much as a whimper. When will they come for you and me? When will we be placed in the **FEMA Death Camps** to silence our cries? **All of this unfolding before our eyes is about to cause a collapse, requiring Martial Law.***

You can clearly see, the inherent mental disorders (Scrupulosity) of our past, was only kept at bay for a short time. The Roman Coliseum of death will reopen for the entertainment of the 1%ers, and be filled with the ones that can't pay their bills or their parent's bills. This is a nightmarish vision only moments away from reality,,, once more.

Sovereign Citizen Movement

The Sovereign Citizen Movement is described as 'a loose group of tax protesters' who claim to be answerable only to their own interpretation of common law. Not subject to any federal or **religious** laws. The FBI states (if you can believe anything they say based on their past) that there are about 100,000 hard core and another 200,000 testing Sovereign techniques. *My thinking is, it is in the millions when you add up all the ones that cheat on their taxes. That's the American way and I bet we are all members of the Sovereign Movement in some way,,, be it small.*

Because this is outside of the powers that can be controlled by the **Big Three**, this group is declared '**a domestic terrorist movement**'. Much like the American Indians were classified as 'savages' making it easier for the Christians' newly formed federal government to slaughter them and take their land. ***When they're all dead,,, there is no one left to complain.***

This is starting to sound like the civil war all over again. ***State's rights to govern themselves.***
September 3, 2016

It was reported that an American Indian burial ground was being destroyed in southern North Dakota, by big business,,, the oil pipe line from Canada to Texas.

Letter to Congress
The bravery of one,,, for us all.

April 4, 2015

A letter carrier (mail man) delivered letters intending to go to every member of Congress, took it upon himself to deliver them by landing his gyrocopter on the White House lawn. When asked why he did not just use the mail service he reportedly said, "They would not read them if I did that." To many, he is another American hero,,, but to the powers,,, he is a terrorist.

It is being reported that the United States Army is about to launch blimps from a design built in WWI with the intent to defend Washington DC. Yes, this is true. Per this report from 12/18/14 the army under the Aerospace Defense Command or the JLENS System will put blimps hovering at 10,000 feet to detect cruise missiles and protect the lords of America. *And you wonder where the tax money goes.*

If this system had been in place our hero mail man would have been shot down and his 500 letters would have gone up in flames over Washington, DC, as another American citizen would have been executed without a trial and due process. *The new American way and we all sit back and say nothing, accepting more murders of American citizens without a trial. It is becoming the new American way and as long as no one complains,,, it's ok.*

October 28, 2015 Update

One of the spy military blimps reportedly worth over one billion **god/notes** (I am not making that number up) broke loose and traveled about 100 miles. It was dragging a long cable taking out power lines along its path. The military had to shoot it down; so, America just lost another billion dollars. *It must be ok.*

Libya 2011

This small country was blown apart by Obama (Christian) as he said, "**it's time for him to go**." Who made him God,,, the pope? Who gave the president that much power? Once more this country (Libya,,, Muslim) did nothing to America (like George W Bush and Iraq) and (Christian America) killed thousands just to get the oil (money),,, like Iraq. *It's Ground Hog Day all over again.* (See the **Big Three** or read the book, *Jesus Christ in Canaan*) as to why.

Today, the country has become a land grab for the local tribes people, (a civil war, as planned by Obama) as the American oil money now comes to the true people in power,,, the **Big Three**. The American taxpayer paid for the war (reportedly 800 billion) and the American oil companies got the oil money and the good Christians got to kill Muslims and now Muslims are killing Muslims. *All part of the master plan,,, (oil, power, money, Christian crusades) if you are still following the gist of this book that is what is leading us to the end of mankind on earth.*

Then ISIS moved into the region and now the oil money is going to fund and disable (or reestablish) this region of the world back to the gods they once had governing them. Their land, their gods, who are we to say it is wrong? *If they want to bring their people back to the 6th century,*

221

with stoning and burning at the stake,,, who are we to say they can't. For some believe this is what the Christians are trying to do,,, bring us all back to the dark ages so as to control us. Back to a much simpler time, when god was in his heaven and they were unaccountable to no man.

The future holds very little promise for the young, as computers take more and more jobs every day, it becomes clear that the de-educated masses will face devastation beyond most people's ability to see. The darkness rumbling just outside our door will be deafening.

The Terracotta Army

When it's all said and done, whoever or whatever is to crawl out of the rocks and crevasses, where life has hung onto this small blue space, what will they find? Will they only find images of the fallen self important leaders that have built monuments to themselves? Will there be rows of carved men standing outside a stone structure; the true final army facing the imaginary self fulfilled religious Armageddon?

The consumption of all resources spent and wasted to appease the gods will be 'plastic' man's legacy. But where will such a monument be built? Will it be in Rome or Washington, D.C. or will the last battle take place on the remains of the ice caps as man faces the inevitable end? *Where is the last stand to be, as* <u>*man*</u> *faces off with Mother Nature, as she enforces Nature's Rights, receiving* <u>*his*</u> *finial Reckoning?*

Some, like myself, believe this self-fulfilled Armageddon of **men** past and present, is with us today and we are witnessing the end of life right now. These religious wars over God to enrich the oil money grabbing bastards of this **mankind** (the Deceivers) will bring about an end to all life,,, the **6th Die Off**. This is not centuries away, this is not decades away, this is not years away,,, this is here now. The end is now and man is moving in slow motion towards the abyss that we all see and know is there.

We are one crisis away from the unraveling of society as Nature's Rights are show to us.

Images of this type are before us if we can find food to eat and water to drink. And of course the will to live in a world of raging heat and pandemic death.

Chapter Nine

Pandemics

The Big Three

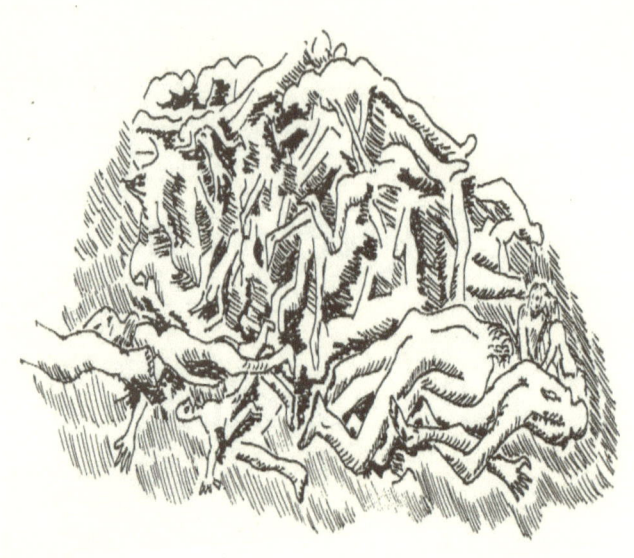

Piles of the dead most of us will never see

What is the **BIG Three** and why are they running everything to the end of life so quickly? Why do they want to see all life as we know it, end? The answer is easy,,, life is of no value to these mentally disturbed people,,, (**god/notes**) and oil is,,, war is,,, power is and many find haven in god. These people are not sane, but are pathological people, hell bent on gathering up as many of these almighty **god/notes** as each one can. Life is a game to them,,, not real and he who has the biggest pile at the end wins. Wins what, I just don't know, for after they have all the **god/notes,** they just give it away in taxes or in charities or no-account relatives. What would make someone want this? Mental disorder or are their brains like that of my dog? When we play tug of war he is constantly moving up on his end of the rope so as to get more and more on his side. He then guards his pile of toys until he becomes bored and then he just walks away. It is just a game to them and all of us in life who don't play,,, pay the price.

If you would like to know more detail on the Big Three, I broke it down in greater depth in the book **Global Financial Super Heating** and the Big Three are as follows;

1. Oil – power
2. War – suppliers
3. Religion – genocide

More to come, see **THE BIG THREE**

Doomsday Clock

Since 1947 the scientists of the world could see what most of us could not,,, the coming of the end of all life.   To some of us today, it is called the **Sixth Die Off**, caused by carbon dioxide, but back in the day,,, just after WWII,,, the ones that helped make the "bomb" envisioned the end of all mankind via nuclear war,,, not climate change. *But for this book I will use the greed of insane man and carbon dioxide, the great planet killer.*

***Nuclear disaster will not come from a war but will come from the collapse of the global almighty god/notes.* Once more the end will come from the paper dollar having no value and radiation from abandoned power plants.**

In that time (1947), these scientists created a time piece to look into the future and track the end of mankind,,, mostly based on politics and a nuclear war. How close to an all out war are we? They called it the **Doomsday Clock**. My view is we need another type of timepiece.

COTE Calendar

If you look at the fluctuations within the environment (we all share) Coming of the End or **COTE** as I like to call it, these adjustment by the scientists would seem to be based on opinion rather than science. So much is due to government propaganda about religion and the justification of war, rather than the facts we are all facing like carbon dioxide pollution in the air, consumption of air and water or global shading, global warming, ice melt off and the consumption of all resources for the allusion of wealth in **god/notes**. *Or the pending global disaster, the collapse of all currency will have on the radioactive power industry. This will bring an end to over 90% of all long term life. Short term life can stand radiation,,, plants,,, bugs,,, some mammals,,, just not most people.* Their Doomsday Clock is now reportedly set at three minutes to midnight. But it has been set at that time before, back in 1949 and 1984. One time it was set at two minutes to midnight in 1953 and when tension between the Soviet Union (now gone) and the United States ended more minutes were placed on the Doomsday Clock, as it rose to twelve minutes before midnight.

If we can remove our eyes from the distractions of the poli-**tricks** and religious hopefuls, we need a new timepiece. One that can more accurately track what is coming based on the past. Unfortunately, there is no past like what is coming at us to base the future on. So I have used the same type of chart in this book on each past event,,, moving forward to present day,,, showing consumption,,, then move the current time, forward to its predictable future outcome in time.

I call this conglomeration of historical facts using logical predictions, the **COTE Calendar**. This takes into consideration certain facts that I believe are overlooked because of all the political influences. The Dooms Day Clock people's eye is still on waging World War 3, this Christian crusade and not on the sciences that keep us all alive. **This thin blue space,,, the only one in the universe that we know of is being crushed into non-existence by man for the insane accumulation of valueless god/notes.**

Zoos

In small places all over the world we people now manage, feed, control and breed the animals displaced from the land, air and sea,,, by humans. The ones that did not get eaten or killed for fun, sport or to get their tusks now get to spend their remaining days in captivity being looked down upon through bars.

These remaining breeding populations live and die without ever knowing the true freedom of running free or soaring in the sky or swimming in the vastness of the seas. They also do not know the death that waits for them; called extinction, part of the **6th die off**.

Zoos have become the last ditched effort or guardians of the lives we people have not yet killed off completely. Now inbreeding is a problem as the end of their breed is to be mutations,,, that is if they can live past the collapse of the worlds **god/notes**. That will cause people to kill and eat them.

Superbugs

February 2015

The Food and Drug Administration (FDA) announced a warning to hospitals and doctors to ensure they clean scopes properly to prevent the spread of CDC, a superbug with no cure... **two dead**.

The Big Three

Who are the Big Three? They are the face of global events that no one seems to quite understand the motives. It is the ones behind the **Big Three** that help explain the motives. But you must understand just who the players are and I would add you as an unaware player,,, a Goy must find out.

1. **War manufactures** cannot make money **god/notes** if there are no wars and religion is the best way for them to make money.
2. **Oil producers** want all the money **god/notes** from its production,,, at any cost and you and your children will pay the price of their gluttony. Cheap oil/gas is not cheap.
3. **Religion**, any religion will do as the catalyst to invade,,, WAR,,, kill the wrong god

people via war,,, get the oil,,, take the **god/notes** enriching themselves. The Christian crusades have been going on enriching the Roman Catholic Church for more than the past 1000 years and are marching on to this date and no one speaks up.

But each one of these cannot do this on their own and must have someone behind the scenes pulling the strings,,, **The String Master.** Now this is nothing so weak as a government or group of governments like the G8 or the G7 they call themselves now days. It is the real money makers behind the closed doors that carve up the world (like Palestine and Libya) enriching themselves.

Governments

The bizarre actions of governments fill the news every day with their unexplained aggression, murder, rape and genocide,,, Iran and Libya are two examples. The unexplained actions of each government have their roots in **The Big Three,** but you must look closer for the underlying power behind their actions.

Christian America is all over the globe killing for the gods, killing for the oil and killing for the holiest of holy's,,, the sacred **god/notes**. Look closely and you will see America is the most destabilizing country in the world and behind most unsettling actions. Don't like a leader,,, kill him. Wrong god,,, kill him, wrong religion,,, kill him.

American Oil companies not getting the profits from the oil,,, kill him and get the oil,,, get the **god/notes**. The string master is behind everything. *But you have to look,,, to see.*

January 3, 2015

Reportedly, the Israeli government has stopped the tax refunds to the Palestine people. Is it because they just don't like giving up other people's money (**god/notes**) or their god does not require it? For the wealth, all wealth in this region is perceived as Jewish money, because those people (Palestine) are just Goyim and as such all Goyim are property of the Jewish people, so murder and genocide is not a crime to them (Jew) or their religion. *For the non Jew (Goy) has a defective soul. They (the gay) and their property belong to the Jewish people.*

March 10, 2015

Reportedly, Christian militias take revenge on Muslims in Central African Republic. They are stating their actions are an **"Ethnic Cleansing,"** exercise in vengeance, an eye for an eye, and they will not stop until ridding the country of Muslims.

*Look closely and you will find this is in the foundations of every branch of Christianity. There is to be but **one god** and that god is to be theirs alone. And when one god is successful in killing off all the other gods, they will turn in on themselves, for those within the ranks,,, just have not been Christian enough to please the higher ups in that religion, so they must be killed as well. History is full of such events. It would seem all gods just can't* *stop the killing and to those of us on the outside, it looks like their god is a devil that they all pray to,,, every religion?*

March 17, 2015

The president of the United States of America, under the puppet masters' guiding hands, has declared tiny **Venezuela as a threat to U.S. security**. What kind of government has this become that it can push us all closer to war with our neighbors? Are they not Christian enough or is it about the oil? *These days it seems America stands for just those things,,, war, oil and religion,,, (Christianity) and all that at any price.*

The disabling of this country has now collapsed the government and its people are starving. This is what Christians do when they do not have all the power. They claim to be peace loving and then they chop off your arms... or your head.

April 24, 2015

The news is full of the latest distractions, as we are all reminded (over and over), that it is allegedly the 100th anniversary of the Turkish massacre of Christian Americans. The Pope, a loving and forgiving man, standing next to God, supposedly tells us all that this atrocity (100 years ago) is genocide. What possible good can come from the Pope's remarks? Oh yeah, I forgot, the Pope is Christian and Turkey is mostly Muslim.

The Pope's remarks are meant to infuriate a new generation of Christian killing soldiers and to help justify the genocide being committed by the Christians now in Iran, Iraq, Syria, Palestine, Egypt, Libya, Tunisia, Yemen, Afghanistan, Pakistan, Israel and Lebanon. *Did you notice… they are all Muslim countries and sense the 1950s Christianity has taken over American government?*

Strange,,, the pot calling the kettle black. **This modern day Christian crusade is pushed along on all sides by all good Catholics; willing to kill for their god,,, but god will not save them from what is to come. Look to the sky's for what we have traded for god/notes.**

June 6, 2015

Turkey is demonstrating against China, over something to do with Muslims in the far west of China. This new friction has most likely something to do with land, God and the **god/note**,,, that's for sure and will enrich the war suppliers. *I thought China just wanted to kill harmless Tibetan Buddhist Monks, for their land, but now they have joined the west and apparently want to kill Muslims as well. Is this to be the new world order? Is this to be the one government I hear so much about these days? It would seem communist China is becoming more aggressive (war like) in the South China Sea and now killing Muslims in the Xinjiang province that it also claims as theirs.*

China is starting to resemble America and America is starting to resemble China, (killing its citizens without a trial). We are seeing the new world order,,, this one global government coming into view. Has it always been there and we just

235

never saw it? If that is true,,, why is it starting to look like everyone and every government is trying to kill all the Muslims in the world?

The part for those of you paying attention is, China is a communist government (a system in which the state plans and controls the economy and a single party holds power) for the good of all. America is also run by a single party (the rich) divided into two parts (republicans and democrats) where the rich choose for us who we can vote for (a single communist party).

A system created by the rich in which the state plans and controls the economy. There is little difference and mostly will be the same under one unelected leader, the string master and Marshall Law, yet to come.

June 18, 2015

Even the Pope is weighing in. Reportedly, stating that humanity's reckless behavior has pushed the planet to the breaking point. *Did someone wake up the gods? Just a suggestion, why don't the Christians stop killing the Muslims for oil and focus on the life giving earth God gave us to care for. Wow! That was strange to say,,, we people all collectively caring for the planet's life giving ingredients. Don't the god people know it's too late? Their war, their Armageddon is coming true and the world will end in fire at the hands of all the religious.*

Via collective intelligence earthlings can finally rise above the ignorance taught to us and passed down generation after generation. Lies taught to us to gain power, (oil) and kill off a race of people must end. Ignorance, bigotry, hatred of people we don't understand to enrich the few is being exposed. We have the power to stop these religious crusades if we will just stop listening to the Deceivers of this world. Only, it is too late.

June 23, 2015

The DARK NET... reportedly, is a location where one goes if they are looking for child pornography. It is said that there are layers of protection to help keep the police from finding the pedophiles. This report states one website gets 500 hits per second. This is becoming a growing trend or it's always been there and it just looks like they are just now coming out of the woodwork.

The question is, if other countries can edit the internet, why can't America? Is it because the Christians leaders in this government and in the church like child porn? *It's against the law, so why not arrest them? Oh yeah,,, it's starting to look like we would have to lock up almost everyone.*

Could this be why the Pope did not turn over the names of the 400 pedophile catholic priests that were kicked out of the church to the police, (per a report from January 17, 2014)?

June 24, 2015

Reportedly, leaks of the most destabilizing country in the world, the United States of America, have come out and another of its oldest allies, France is being spied on by the U.S.A. Why would this federal government need to spy on its allies?

They're all Christian, so it can't be religion. So what is it they fear? *I don't know what is worse,,, that they do it or that they do it so poorly. Maybe they just don't care if they get caught. Flaunting their power over the world is part of the fun of being the string master. It says clearly, 'I don't care what you think',,, but their our ally,,, we need to care.*

July 31, 2015

An Israeli extremist group set fire to a home in what remains of the country of Palestine, (land the Jews have not stolen) killing an infant. Our American tax dollars pour in to support Israel and its murdering occupying Jewish government. *This clearly is ok with the American people, for it is their tax dollars that are killing Muslims via the Jews and no one in America speaks out against this.* **'Let my enemy kill my enemy'** *is a system that works well for all religions.* God is not behind the land grab or killing, it is man and his religion.

October 9, 2015

Revenge Stabbings... Reportedly, the **(occupier) Jewish Israeli government** is facing retaliations for its crushing treatment of the Palestinian people (Jews murdering Muslims with Christian dollars). Surprisingly, to this Jew government, the genocide of a race of people so they can have their land and the wealth derived from it, is met with resistance, making them (the Jews) terrorists.

I am sure the **occupying Jewish government,** believes the Palestinian Muslim people should stop complaining about having their homes taken and their people killed. After all the Jewish religion believes the Palestine people are here on earth to serve them and per their religion the Jews can do whatever they want. The Palestine people are murdered and pushed further out of their country and into the sea with the blessing of the American government. *How do the Jews justify these acts of genocide and ethnic cleansing? Oh, yeah, they are God's people and have a right to kill all the goyim if they want.* **It is written into their religion.**

Only if we expose these teachings for what they are can we hope to stop a future filled with more land grabs and genocide. Mass exposure of these atrocities found within all religions is our only hope as our collective knowledge grows.

Regardless of how people wakeup to the lies found within all religions, the crash of the global **god/notes** will bring about a pandemic. It will be at that time the true effects of the loss of air come into play.

Nature's Rights

Chapter Ten

The
Point Of No Return

**Supper Heated Wasteland
Earth**

It's at this point that I turn and try to look forward in order to see what is to come for every living thing on this planet and the death that is to come. From what direction will death come and how can each one of us prepare for the inevitable as we cross this point in time? **The next 100 years or,,, Four Generations,,, the millennium children and their decedents. What will they live to see?**

The larder that you have stocked up food and water in to carry you through hard times will not be enough, as our ignorance is shown to each one of us via these times that are yet to come. It will be made clear that the Free Market System or communism or socialism is not free; taught ignorance has a price.

To make things clear, the Free Market System is a phrase that's true meaning is, **"I can do anything to the land, air, water and all life in the pursuit of taking as much paper with ink on it as I can from you. Then you can pay to clean up the mess I make."**

Communist and socialist governments do this as well. You must keep your eye on the one

pulling the strings behind all leaders. The rich will eat well for a time, but wherever they go, the masses will follow, leaving death on all sides.

Yet, this Free Market System is not totally responsible for the upcoming dilemma, the one just at our door step; the blame is shared by others. The others that hold much of the responsibility wear many hats and all of them look up to one single entity in the sky. This imaginary creature, individual, being, or thing is sometimes jointly referred to as god and all the actions of the religious are somehow justified in his name. The rape, murder, theft of wealth, genocide and destructions of the life giving elements found only on earth, that belong to all of us, are taken for the benefit of a few,,, in god's name.

Then there are all the gadget people, the ones that must have one of everything; a new thingamabob every week, as they race to the edge of the cliff, trying to keep up with the Joneses or get ahead. It's those that will be hardest hit, for they know nothing of life and the hardships necessary to survive. They live in an imaginary world of endless games and resources and endless imaginary wealth to be taken. *They will be the first to go and most likely at their own hand for they cannot adapt.*

These are the same people that are in 100% denial over the future. They believe global warming is a natural occurring event; and they press on, pushing the rest of us over that cliff,,, all for that love of paper with ink on it,,, the almighty **god/notes**.

Several questions come to mind at this point and they are as follows:

1. How do we stop what is to come?
2. Can anyone wake up the leaders of the world?
3. Is man's need for an old man in the sky to guide him, ever to end so we all can stop killing each other,,, for God's sake?
4. What can I do to prepare for what is to come?

The thing to remember is,,, there is no quick fix. Things are not going to continue as they are without some very major changes. To me the answers to these questions are clear:

1.) We cannot fix this,,, it is coming and coming hard and fast. The short term future is black and there will be no food to eat. So like all starving creatures we turn upon ourselves. **Cannibalism, for the first generation, is to return as the land is cleared of all living things.**

2.) No one can see the future if we don't look at it. The leaders are paid for by the String Master to look the other way and only care about money. None of them will guide us to the promised land,,, for we had the promised land and now have destroyed it. **It looks like man's gods led us from the promised land, to the hell that is to come,,, and come very soon.**

3.) The fear is these gods will be with us forever, (until the end of man or the end of mans gullibility), as man cannot function without filling this father figure complex of Scrupulosity. **Clearly to the intelligent, religion is a mental disorder.**

Man must face this crippling disease of the mind if ever man should have any hope of short term survival.

    4.) The list of preparations is not long and will be provided in detail at the end of this book. **It truly depends upon when man collective understands all aspects of the future that will determine the course of the future.**

What Is To Come?

Currency – god/notes

    Everything is riding on the concept of paper with ink on it, as having value,,, the almighty **god/notes**. But today, I estimate 80% of the **god/notes** in circulation are made of blue sky, air, numbers on a computer or piece of paper,,, not real currency. When the crash comes,,, and it will come, the banks, and the government will have nothing to hand out,,, currency. A full 80% is not real,,, not even so much as a worthless paper **god/note**.

    Before the industrial age and the creation of paper money, coin of the realm was real gold and silver. **Something you could hold and trust as real.** Coins once made of precious metals and valuable everywhere in the world, are today made of junk and have little or no value; **coins are the pretense of value**. Think what can you buy with a coin?

    The crash of currency is all around us if we would just take the time to look. America is doing all it can to drive down other countries' currency to lift its own,,, but it is nothing more than paper with ink on it and like coins,,, paper money is **the pretense of value**.

The ones that realize this and pull their heads out of the sand, out of this dreamland fantasy, will be the ones that survive for the short term,,, the first awakening millennium children. Your blind trust, your blind faith is what is driving the rich to become richer. **You can bet some of them are doing something you are not to prepare for what is to come. For them, will it be enough?**

Water

The unchecked growth of the population of the planet requires more and more, clean fresh water to drink and to grow more and more food. Man will die within seven days so I am told, without water.

All across the globe we are seeing record droughts that are causing farmers to be unable to grow food. Less food means the price we pay will require more **god/notes**. This will mean that the rich will eat and the poor will not – **as always has been the case.**

Rivers, lakes and streams are drying up and most importantly, farmers are pulling water from the earth that has been in storage for over 10,000 years (aquifers), this will soon be gone. Now, add to that mix the pollutions across the globe and water is very high on the list of disasters we all are just about to face. **People will leave the polluted water behind and head for clean water,,, yours. But the mix of toxins will have no boundaries and** will **follow them as this world of clean water grows ever smaller and more valuable. Death from the lack of water or from poisoned water is very near for everyone.**

For some, if they can't buy it,,, they will come and take it,,, and major wars over water will begin. It may come under the pretense of a war for God,,, but like oil, killing for God has other prices.

Canada has 31,752 lakes larger than three square kilometers and is not a peaceful country for it has openly engaging in wars against Muslims for their land and their oil with America. If there is a country that would be invaded for its resources it would be Canada and they could not defend themselves. So America will have to step in and help,,, taking its full share of water and, of course, oil. **Those lakes would be pumped dry to feed a thirsty nation (America). It will not take long and that water will be gone as well. Canada will be invaded from all sides as their land heats up in the future global warming.**

Food

As the new hungry and/or starving, overpopulated regions of the world use up all their resources, (or those resources are destroyed by outside religions i.e. Syria vs. Germany) they will look to the ones that did not consume them or have resources. Those that took care of their land and their water (one example Canada) will be inundated by the migrating masses from all sides like the American Indians were.

When they arrive at your door step, all they (the immigrants) will want is,,, your food,,, your water,,, your home,,, and some will want your job and willing to work for less. Then they will want their god to rule your land as he did in their abused, abandoned, and tortured land. Only you and your god stand in their way of a better life,,, your life. *Even the dead American dream is better than life in their old country destroyed by one god or another to enrich the few.*

When the hungry amass on your borders, no country has enough bullets to hold them back. They will get what they want and their god will rule over yours. As for you and yours,,, if they have not killed you,,, if they have not eaten you,,, you can live in the sewers as people did in Poland when the **German Christians** took over their country in WWII.

These types of adjustments are what is in the future of every man, woman and child that did not prepare.

Air

There are many things that will kill man but little attention is given to the air we breathe. After all, there is so much of it that one could never believe we could run out. What was that I just said,,, **run out of air**???

How can we run out of air? Oh yeah, we cut down all the trees that make air and burn them converting the air into carbon dioxide (a poison) that ends up in the sea. We created engines that convert air into carbon monoxide (a poison) that ends up in the air we breathe as well as the sea. Both poison gases sink down to the earth were we live and breathe causing new levels of death.

Allegedly, jets must now lower their flight path height to keep the engines running and the planes in the thicker air. We are running out of air,,, good air and our lungs are becoming damaged by the junk we are putting out there in place of air, (poison invisible gas).

Global Warming

As the planet warms (as it is now doing) so will the oceans (as they are now doing) and with that will come ever stronger changes in the jet streams that circle the globe (that is happening today). The hot air will push up into colder regions and push that cold air south, in places like the eastern part of North America (as it is happening today). The heating up of these great bodies of water will continue as we are told by the Deceivers of the world that there is no such thing as Global Warming. Reversing these affects from carbon dioxide will take thousands of years if left up to Mother Nature.

October 14, 2015

Hurricane Patricia, hit Mexico as a category Five, the highest on record,,, ever,,, produced in the Pacific Ocean. Reportedly, the mountains broke it apart but I also believe the lower amount of air helped to kill this destructive giant of storms.

It was reported that this giant storm was only 15 miles wide from the center. Not 150 miles wide as you would expect a massively strong storm like this to be. The power was there (cat 5) but the strength was not. I believe the reason for this is because of the lesser amount of air circulating the planet. These storms have less girth behind them, less punch because there is less air.

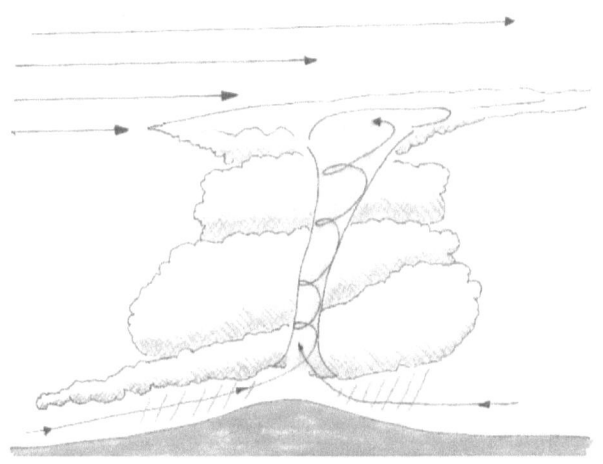

The effects of a warmer and dryer planet are all around us, if only we will look. The big question is, how do we survive,,, how do you and your family make it to see the next generation live?

The Short Term Solution

Clearly, the problem we all face is not the earth, the seas or the air, but the one creature that has risen to the top of the animal food chain. Yet, this creature is not just an animal,,, no, no,,, it is much worse,,, it is a human addiction to money. This creature thinks it is smart and in some ways it is, but nonetheless, the imaginary gods and the imaginary fortunes made, come at a price and what a price it will be.

The human quest to gain as many **god/notes** as one can carry back to their castle is something I witness in my pet dogs. The quest, goal, ambition or **game** is to get as many toys as possible in a pile and guard them,,, then he will just walk away, bored with this game. **Much like the rich do at the end of their lives, they give it away,,, for it has no value.**

When we play tug of war, his aggression is not just to out pull me in this game of tug of war,,, but to move his way up the rope until he has it all. When he wins the game he proudly walks back to his bed,,, his home,,, toys with it for a little while then,,, he abandons it,,, giving it away by leaving behind to whoever else may want it and play this game,,, **wealth**.

The human animal shows every sign of aggression to fill his nest with as much as he can carry (**god/notes**) for the future or the game, and when he no longer wants it, or reaches old age, he just gives it away. I personally have never understood this money (greed) game,,, and at this age I never will. *I call this the DOG Factor.*

Nonetheless, when we no longer can find value in the almighty **god/notes**, (paper with ink on it) we will all become the human animal and we will kill to feed our own. The predominate thought will be "My life is more valuable than yours," and in that thinking, I can justify taking what is yours,,, including your food, your water, your house, your land, your job and your life.

Therefore, the following is a subject most people do not want to look at or talk about,,, but it is there before us all,,, just waiting,,, rumbling outside our door.

Cannibalism

The following is a very dark subject for most of us to consider let alone vision in our minds as possible,,, but possible it is, and we must prepare for it. You may find it too repulsive to ever consider, but others will do this with ease and it will, because it's easier with time. It will be those willing to adapt via starvation that will survive this first stage of the upcoming 6th die off.

Donner Party

In 1846-47 eighty seven members of a group of **Mormons** set out to cross the Sierra Nevada and became trapped in the mountains that winter. Of the initial 87 men, women, and children, 48 survived,,, many of them had done so by eating the dead,,, humans.

Mormons consider themselves Christians
Pointing this out is not to bring shame upon their religion but to show how quickly we will turn on each other for food. It should be noted,,, not all did eat human flesh,,, it's a matter of discipline,,, that most of us do not have.

Ask anyone and they will tell you, there are just too many people on the earth. This planet cannot sustain this number of people and fulfill the greed and aggression for the **god/notes** at any price. Something is going to break,,, something is going to give way and man will be on our dinner plate.

Get used to the idea,,, after all we are just made up of meat and the Christian religion believes this is ok to consume meat from man. ***"Eat my flesh drink my blood" and they still do, to this very day. Eating humans will be as easy for the Christians as killing.***

Now, that should not be surprising to you for as we move through this supposed prosperous time, people are eating people around the world now and have never stopped. This is not just wild savages from the past of distance lands, but today.

When the Czar and/or Tsar of Russia lived like gods on earth (**Orthodox Christianity**) and the poor, if they were to survive, learned to eat human flesh. Now this was just approximately little over 100 years ago. These people of power ruled their part of Asia until they were removed and killed and their power taken.

The French did much the same thing and publicly lopped off their heads. In Europe these kings of the land that have been inbreeding with each other for over 500 years, are the last to survive as I understand. And people support them.

Today, as we see just the very few accumulate all the wealth, these new kings of cash (**god/notes**) soon will start to live on estates and dictate to the underlings, we Goyim, and they will rule once more. The kings of cash, the royalty of the **god/notes** will be the new rulers of the land. The only thing is, we just will not see this time last, for the planets resources will fail the system and the cash will collapse.

The new kings of the earth can hide behind their golden doors as others like them have in the past. Only the migrations of the starving will be before them pounding at their doors. Starvation is the future for all of us but the rich and the smart,,, *for the short term*.

Some estimate **every surviving man, woman and child must eat at least five people** to end the immediate starvation crisis before us all. Now you may think I am nuts to say that, but it is what the human animal does. To survive, eating people is just around the corner.

So one of the first things one must do to prepare for the future is develop a taste for human flesh. At the scent of cooking food they will be climbing thru your windows to get to you and it, so you will have to kill or be killed.

Learning how to preserve meat by drying it,,, human junkie,,, will keep the family going.

Abandon your Mansion for a squalor lifestyle, for the rich will be the first to see the revenge of the starving. The homes of the rich (the McMansion) will be invaded, food stolen and inhabitants killed and eaten,,, then their mansions burned to the ground for fun. The full bellies will dance for joy around the embers of the rich and then the starving will move on to the next home,,, the next McMansion.

I estimate the first years of this crash will see one quarter of the world's population disappear and this easing will suggest a return to the new normal. But do not be deceived, for the super heating is just about to get much worse.

Defense of One's Castle

When the markets crash and the **god/notes** have no value other than burning them for heating or cooking food,,, defense is what should be on your mind. Once more, if you are rich and live like a king,,, they will find you and eat your family. *They will most likely come as the face or justification of god,,, or a religion representing god and that (religion) will help the masses to kill the rich.*

Smaller groups of people (tribes) will fare better than those that rely on the police or the military to defend them (if there will be such a thing). Those people (police/military) will not be able to protect their families and work for **god/notes** of no value. They will most likely be home doing the same thing you are,,, guarding the castle,,, the home front,,, keeping the home fires going. *Or they will move their families into the FEMA death camps and work for the **military currency** - for there is safety in those guarded camps. That is if you know how to work the guillotine, as the keepers do and not the kept.*

I estimate the first months to be the hardest, for most people don't have one week's worth of food stored away. Most are like my ex-wife who would buy food on the way home each night from work. Those are the ones ill equipped to survive in this future of strained resources.

For the most part, there will be no work, no jobs, no money, no food and no water. Only madness on the streets, as **Martial Law** tries to control the starving masses from their golden towers. After those that relied on electronics, relied on the illusion of society discover it gone, well some will not be able to adapt and willing death will become the only way out of this new madness called humanity.

Unless you can adapt to these changes, your body will feed the new smaller mankind, the new society, the new world order. The good old days are gone for good,,, there is no going back. Society is but an illusion of order that will disappear with empty bellies, hunger and starvation.

Coin of the Realm

The smart ones will make it for a time (depending on the state or government) and they will have diversified their **god/notes** to tangibles. What is there that you can exchange for goods and services? What do you have that I can use to exchange with others and they will trust it and accept it? *Those that prepare will survive,,, those that do not prepare will starve and be eaten.*

Silver

Currency, paper with ink on it or **god/notes** (regardless of the country) will have no value. Now the dying governments of the world will offer new **god/notes** in exchange, as they have in the past. You are given so many days to do the exchange and any time after that date, your old saved money is of no value.

That action will mean the government does not have to honor the old bad money sitting in a drawer or buried in a can some place in your back yard; their responsibility to honor it, is gone. Their new money is more valuable, because their debt of responsibility is now reduced by disvaluing the old money.

As it is today, when you save money, you put cash away and it shrinks in value,,, per the government's plan (5% per year). That is why they push you to save money,,, it makes their newly presented money more valuable. If you spent yours,,, putting it into circulation, theirs drops in value.

The suckers that kept their wealth in bonds or the banks or the **Shark Markets** are to be the ones on the outside looking in. As they will not be able to adapt to a lawlessness or lack of society and will fall to the wayside and be eaten.

Now, don't go nuts with blocks of silver for the amount of its value of exchange will need to be small. Old silver coins, even though they are not pure silver (dirty silver), have more value because they can be exchanged for smaller items like food. *These coins are sometimes found to be 40 to 60% silver and sometimes called dirty silver.*

Now please note; I did not say anything about gold do to its cost. Its cost is too high and will be hard to exchange on small daily basic needs.

Nature's Rights

Chapter Eleven

What the Hell Is Going On?

One Million Years Ago

Over 50% Gone and disappearing fast

It's about the Air STUPID!!!

Where are we now?
2017

Land is disappearing before our eyes and with it the ability to **grow food** (rice, corn, potatoes, grain, wheat, and so on.) for the ever growing population of the world. *Remember when one source of food is gone, that will put a strain on all the others sources and run up the price.*

Louisiana is "sinking" into the Gulf of Mexico. Reportedly, as of 2014 the state has lost 2000 square miles of land. I believe that there is much more land disappearing than they tell us and much of the ability to grow other foods, like shrimp and fish also is gone for good. The highest point the state is 535 feet, and at its lowest point it is 8 feet under sea level. *With the melting of the worlds ice you can see 8 feet under sea level is not a good place to build your home,,, yet people do believing in the system...fools!*

Due to the rich bottomland from the Mississippi river, Louisiana has reportedly eight million acres for farming land and produces corn, sugarcane, and soybeans. It is ranked 3rd in this nationals rice production.

As this state continues to be losing its wetlands, additionally due to saltwater intrusion, 25 square farming miles are lost per year, as of 2014 and will be much faster as time goes on. Each year that is less and less land to grow food for an ever growing world population.

We are standing at or have pasted the tipping point of our food production and its production is only going to go down. The river that feeds this state is allocated in the future (by other states) to consume all the water long before it ever gets to the Gulf of Mexico. The more fresh water removed from this region the more salt water is going to leach in to wells and aquifers.

It has been reported that carbon dioxide is causing the breakdown of lime rock; which causes sinkholes as well as removing all the fresh water. These sinkholes are just one more slow-motion death of this state as towns and roads disappear into the sea.

Gulf of Mexico

The **Mekong River** starts in the Tibetan Mountains, which its people are now under the control of China. It works its way south through Thailand, Laos, and Cambodia then finally through the lower part of Vietnam; reportedly, because each country is using more and more of the river to grow food and care for its people.

Asia is in a drought (2016) like California is and so 15% of the Middle East and South Asia (India, Afghanistan, Iran and Pakistan) are suffering. This is the worst drought since 1971. Another ten percent of the population is at risk of starvation and will be on the move.

Now stop and think; when China needs more water its government could just divert the Mekong River water from the Tibetan Plateau to the Yellow River. If it can do that to one river it can do that to the Ganges River starving India and its people. ***Wars over water will start in the first generation of this new millennium.***

Vietnam is also suffering in the worst drought in 90 years by some reports. It too is experiencing salt water leaching into its fields where fresh water once rained down upon them.

South Korea is producing over 20% less rice since its hay day of the late 70s, because of the population and its industrial growth. Regardless, it has more people and less food. The recent high point of production was hit in the year of 2013 and regardless of the cause; rice production has declined for the past three years.

The people of North Korea, as we know are starving and their required height for its military is now recently lowered. When you do not feed a child, the child is stunted.

All these countries have relied on each other to share the water. As the drought continues, all water in the world will be diverted. Wars over water,,, major wars will see millions killed. Many have the bomb and will use it to save their people.

Part ONE of the 6th Die Off GOVERNMENT COLLAPSE

The big question should be; how will it start and what will it be like for each one of us? This is a question I have struggled to understand. For most people I speak to on this point,,, they don't want to talk about it. "I don't want to be around the dooms day people." is how they view any discussion on this future point. I think they will be the first to look to god for the answers and "the earth will end in a fiery ball" and they accept that.

The first wave of the dead to leave the earth will have to face no water and starvation. Water pollution to feed the rich **god/notes** will leave most people no choice but to leave vast regions of land. In China they're called "Dead Zones" and these people will cross the planet like the cancer they produce and the death they bring is coming.

The first to leave will be the nomadic rich, taking their bags of **god/notes** with them leaving the poor behind to struggle with the filth left behind. We can see this today in 2016, as corporations are leaving for tax breaks and the rich are giving up their USA citizenship.

The debt run up by the traitorous leaders will show the world just how valueless those **god/notes** truly are, as they drop to their true value,,, nothing. The next financial collapse will be the big one; there will be no bailout, for there is no more borrowed money in the government's banks. It was all used up in 2007 and 2008.

The madness that will ensue after these first coming days will have no end, no bailout and in those first weeks, those first months, people will lose their jobs and run out of money for food. At first, all bills will not be paid but water and food. They will keep their power on until there is no money for it.

By the sixth month, major businesses and stores will close and banks will collapse, as they did in 2008. Only this time there will be no bailout. Inner cities will see marauding mobs looting, stealing anything they can to trade for food. These will become the new war zones.

History of South Africa

It will be at the point when local law enforcement cannot stop the mobs of starving. In some places, the National Guard will be called out to defend the streets. That will not be enough in the first days, and the ever growing mobs will move to any perceived location that has been un-hit by this man made tragedy. Only then, vigilante justice will be called upon to defend your home.

As one country falls so will another, for it has been some time now (over 100 years), that each country has been supporting the other and their ever falling **god/notes**. Like one drunk leaning on the other, this collapse will bring them all down and their borders will melt away for good.

Martial Law

Military law will rule the land with an iron fist at first, giving the pretense of control, but there will be no controlling these mobs of starving. From city to city, if you cannot defend your home, the mobs will kill you. For most, they will pack up and leave looking for food and water. *You see city dwellers rely on each other to live. Millions stacked upon each other, all without food without water. You can see it will not take long.*

The perceived value of country life will draw the masses to the rural communities. The farmers will do their best to defend the land, adding the corpses to the compost pile and saving the good meat for the smokehouse. They will not go hungry until the next bigger wave comes, (part two of the 6th Die Off).

It will become every man for themselves. That is when the FEMA Death Camps will open, to "hold the displaced" per the creators of these camps. Why are they to be held behind three layers of barbed wire,,, facing the inside if it is to help the displaced? Retreating to these camps will not stop what is to come, for the camps are for the processing of the rioting, starving ones.

America has prepared for this with a military government within the freely elected one we believe to exist. This military government that is working with the C.I.A., will ultimately rule these camps. They are to dispose of the unwanted by allegedly, cutting off their heads. *Yes, American citizen will be executed for trying to feed their families in this government society collapse.*

This military government living and working within our society is in itself a separate society of people that for all intents and purposes, act like occupiers. They are the **Occupying Military** in America. We have seen them take over other governments, permitting so called free elections. This **Occupying Military** here now live within, their own cities, their own governing bodies and their own laws, their own currency and even their own nuclear power plants.

They created their own currency, called Allied Military Currency in WWII (AMC). Each country Germany, Austria, France, Italy and Japan had their own currency, and control paper money printed in these **occupied countries**.

When the global **god/notes** fail across the world, new military money will become the cone of the realm, as your paper money will have no value. For the short term, their system of military money will still work,,, yours will not. Your 401k will have no value, as the shark market will be there only symbolically. *You might have money there,,, but you can't get to it,,, for the government will not permit that. You have your money, your wealth to feed your family, don't be silly, you have not wealth, money is of no value,,, remember. All corporations' assets will belong to the government.*

As bad as it will be in America, it will be much worse in other countries; as this opportunity to take advantage of the disadvantaged will be too much to pass up. Killing for god and religion will take over. The world will see ethnic cleansing as it is in Syria, where this is called a civil war,,, but it is really about religion and power over the land ($$$), *one god over another,,, perpetrated by the power behind the war suppliers.*

Total dead to this date (2015) is questionable, but some reports are at 55,000 and the displaced are estimated at 9 million; placing tremendous burdens (food water) on the neighboring countries that now must feed and clothe these people. The strain on their economy is bringing Europe to a standstill as all these countries show the world,,, they don't want them either.

This is the future to come for us all, when all **god/notes** crash and over 7.7 billion people must face uncontrolled human growth and exploitation of resources. *Like it or not,,, Nature's Rights will prevail over us all and only a very few will survive the short term.*

Ten years into this time, I estimate 20 to 30 percent of the population will be eliminated, as the migrating invade from all sides. The population will decrease by 1.5 billion to 2.3 billion people by 2028 - 2030.

The United Nations has predicted a reduction of the planets population to just over 6 billion people by the year 2100. *That is 4 generations from now. That is you,,, your kids,,, your grand kids,,, and your great grand kids will see this reduction if you live that long.* That optimistic view shows a reduction of 1.7 billion, but I predict the number of this first wave of death in the first part of the 6th Die Off to be 2.3 billion. I also believe that it will take no more than 10 years from the collapse of the **god/notes**,,, not 85.

It will move very fast across the land. Neighbor will kill neighbor, as was done in Bosnia and Herzegovina, that genocide killed an estimated 104 thousand people because of religion.

Killing for god will overtake the world during this time. If you are to survive, you must insure you are on the right side of religion. Pick a strong one.

Within the law, creating and funding the FEMA Death Camps, one religion was included within the law,,, it is Christianity.

Part TWO of the 6th Die Off HEAT

The full effects of **Global Financial Super Heating** as laid out in a book of the same name will cover the globe in a matter of days and within weeks everyone will know of its true meaning.

Venezuela is a perfect example of one country in economic collapse and its people will leave, because they cannot afford to feed their families with worthless God/Notes.

1. The United States declares Venezuela a national security threat and begins to topple its leaders and bring down its economy. ***Once more,,, America did this to them for their oil.***

2. This is an oil based economy and the price of oil in July 2016, is now hovering in the low $30s. Not good when their government was enjoying $100.00 per barrel before. They spent it like it was going to go to $200.00 per barrel,,, as predicted,,, or hoped by the super rich.

3. Their currency has fallen through the floor and the Bolivar dollar is now worth much less than one US penny.

4. Default on their loans is clearly part of their past and this will continue in their future. They will become isolated from other countries as this region is forced into chaos.

5. Typical power struggle ensues for control of this sinking ship.

6. As is always the case, the little people pay the price and now there is a food shortage that includes milk, flour, eggs and potatoes.

Keep in mind now this is but one country out of 196, unless you discount Taiwan, as does the USA.

Most Americans are one paycheck away from the street by some accounts and it is not going to take much to push us all over the cliff that is just before us. **Why is that important?**

Every country has moved from a currency backed with a tangible like gold and silver, has enjoyed the illusion of the value of its paper currency. They have, for some time now, been tricking its citizens. This is the reason the united states dollar added 'note' to the bills and then the word 'god',,, hence the name **god/note**.

Economists have for some time now, predicted the next collapse in the financial markets around the world. The 2008 bailout only postponed the inevitable market crash. The next crash is to be much worse than 2007 and 2008…. much worse. It will be a downward spiral, pulling every country into its vortex of death. **What will it be like and why is paper money a concern?**

In conjunction with Part One of the 6th Die Off, economies around the world will see their **god/notes** fall apart and become worth their true value,,, nothing. Global runs on banks and collapse of stock markets will cause life savings to disappear overnight. Only those that invested in real tangibles (gold and silver) will eat. Human life will have no value, but as a food source. *It will become very cheap indeed.*

Money will have no value,,, therefore, people will not be traveling via the air and plane travel will grind to a halt. Only a few military plans will be in the air, paid for with military **god/note** money. The lack of jet pollution in the upper atmosphere,,, (those contrails making the sky grey), will be gone and the sky will turn blue once again.

The sun will show its true brilliance as it begins to heat things up very quickly.

The earth will keep getting warmer and warmer every year. We set new records, but this year 2015 – 2016, was the first time the North Pole did not freeze over. The newly exposed black water of the North Pole will absorb the heat from the sun and melt what is left of the ice all that much quicker. Some estimates are between 20 and 30 years for a complete melt off; **or by the beginnings of the second generation.**

This is one of the great air conditioner of the planet. Without it, the center of the earth will heat up all that much faster as the South Pole melts. Remember there is no turning back from this as each year it will get hotter and hotter.

My prediction is, when the global dollar collapses the super heating will happen very quickly. The ice of the world will disappear much faster than the experts predict because of the crash of the **god/notes**.

Clean water to drink and grow food will disappear as we pull it out of the ground at alarming rates. This will expedite the mass migration of the starving. Many will dry up in the heat and mummify.

But this heat will not immediately kill everyone. There are parts of the planet untouched by the destruction of man and these temporary pockets of isolation will now be in high demand. Like the American Indians,,, the U.S. government will declare a race and religion. Then they will declare those that do not worship that god to be savages or terrorist and kill them and take their land and water. Remember they have done this before.

But that will not save us from the next part of the 6th Die Off. This will happen when the mad dash to grab hold of life sustaining resources starts.

Part THREE of the 6th Die Off NUCLEAR

When all is said and done, mans greed (addiction to money and power) to obtain riches and wealth and the complete disregard for others and the planet that gives everything life, will be at the root of its demise. ***Worshipers of the god/note will leave their indelible mark for a very long time.***

Cheap power (oil, gas, **nuclear**), has an unseen price (hidden from most of us, but not hidden from the 1%ers), to be paid and that bill will come due soon after the collapse of the global dollar. The carnage that is to follow will have no regard for life and little will survive this next stage of Die Off.

Part Three of the 6th Die Off will began when the almighty **god/notes** of the world are discovered to have no value. The next big financial crash that is but a short few moments away will reveal the true damage done by man and hidden by the Deceivers. The days of plenty are truly gone and the future of part three of the 6th Die Off can only be cleaned up with time. The remnants of greed will cover the earth for over 5000 years until it sinks into the mud of time.

It would make sense that the military of the United States would have a separate form of financial currency to insure theirs is not linked to all others that is crashing. The FEMA relocation camps (or death camps) will need to house the less than 1% of the United States military (that have not abandoned the government to care for their families) and process the combative element that will come seemingly from all sides.

As part one and part two of the Die Off are unfolding, they will be setting up this final part three of the 6th Die Off. Because money will have no value, the great abandonment will unfold and the irreversible destruction will began in earnest.

Because the death of the global **god/note** has occurred, the oil industry will just walk away from its ageing facilities. The average pipeline's lifespan is 33 years, and most are 30 years old as of 2016. There are tens of thousands of abandoned oil and gas wells in the Gulf of Mexico. The BP oil spill sent endless black muck covering thousands of square miles, causing endless death as they poured millions of dollars into trying to stop it (and that was but one). When each one of these deep abandoned pipes rusts away, they will in their turn release their uncontrolled death into the air and water. Some will burn for decades, but that will be nothing compared to the long term devastation to come from the **radiation** industry and its abandonment because of the crashing global dollar.

The life expectancy of a nuclear power plant is about 30 years (as of 2016, they are calming 35 to 40 years is the new life span since they just moved the goal post) and then it is to be dismantled and/or abandoned. There are many of these plants at risk when the sea levels rise, so these abandoned nuclear power plants will be under water, soon.

Nuclear power reactors around the world, reportedly number over 430; with over 60 more soon to come on line. This does not include military insulations, atomic bombs or war ships and submarines all holding the same fate for us all,,, death,,, used or not. *This is one of the longest legacies to be left of man. If any life is to survive, their DNA must have the qualities to overcome radiation's devastating effects on the mammal body. There are people that can withstand massive amounts of radiation,,, but can they reproduce after exposure?*

When the collapse of the **god/note** occurs, these corporations will have no money to pay people to properly close down these facilities and pay to store the unused radioactive material, (if there is such a thing as properly store radioactive material). **The current plan now is too temporarily store our unwanted radioactive material ON SITE. When the plants close at the end their life cycle,,, 30 to 40 years or for many a maximum of 10 years from 2016,,, these temporary storage locations will become permanent. That is until they all rot and split open. Radioactive material is as of December 2016 (2026), coming on shore in the state of Washington from the Fukushima power plant.**

One such example of our (America) inability to contain radiation can be found in the Hanford

Site, sometimes called the Hanford Project or my favorite, the Hanford Nuclear Reservation. Don't you think 'reservation' has such a nice peaceful native tone to it? Natural and save,,, but it is anything but. For over 73 years this government has worked to contain the radiation (and other unknowns) leaking from this plant and to date, completely failed. This death is now leaking into the water table and into the Columbia River, unabated by the American military government's best efforts. *When I say best efforts I mean they did nothing but spend money.*

From 1946 to 1958 nuclear devices were detonated at Bikini Atoll or the Bikini Island. Reportedly, a total of 23 radioactive bombs were exploded over this picturesque site. The native people of this site were thankfully, removed first and placed on a strip of jagged rock with no beaches still to this day under the care and feeding of the United States.

To this day,,, 70 years later,,, the indigenes people of these islands cannot return home. With our best efforts,,, this land is still not safe for humans. You do see, don't you,,, it can't be contained, no matter what lies we are being told. **There are thousands of these places across the world.**

When there is no money to pay people to work in these soon to close nuclear power plants, they, the 1%ers, will just walk away (as they have in the past) and we will be plunged into darkness,,, **no electricity**. There is but less than one percent of the population in the military to protect us from the invasion of the starving and the battle that is to come from that front. They will not have the time or resources to run these plants let alone dispose of the radiation properly,,, (if there ever was a proper way) it will not happen. **This radiation will seep into the ground water, the rivers and lakes and into the air we breathe.**

To find a temporary safer place inhabit and to better understand just how this will unfold, you need to understand how the weather patterns will distribute the radioactive material across the globe. It will come via aquifers, rivers, the oceans and by air, but will also be carried by the short lived creatures we share this thin blue space with,,, birds,,, fish,,, infected rats and people.

The following map shows the approximate locations of known nuclear power plants, storage facilities and improper dumping of nuclear waste on land. **Please note, that this map is incomplete and based on only information we are being told. It does not include military facilities and dumping and/or storage.**

As you can see the majority of these nuclear wastes dump sites (that we know of) are across the northern hemisphere of the planet. As part three of the 6th die off unfolds in the next few decades, where will the slowly disappearing and polluted air carry this unseen death?

Sothern parts of Argentina and Chile would at first appear to be safer places to live. Yet I believe this radiation will have no boundaries and will cross into all continents. I believe that the remote South America will hold the most protection from this death only because it has been mostly free of people.

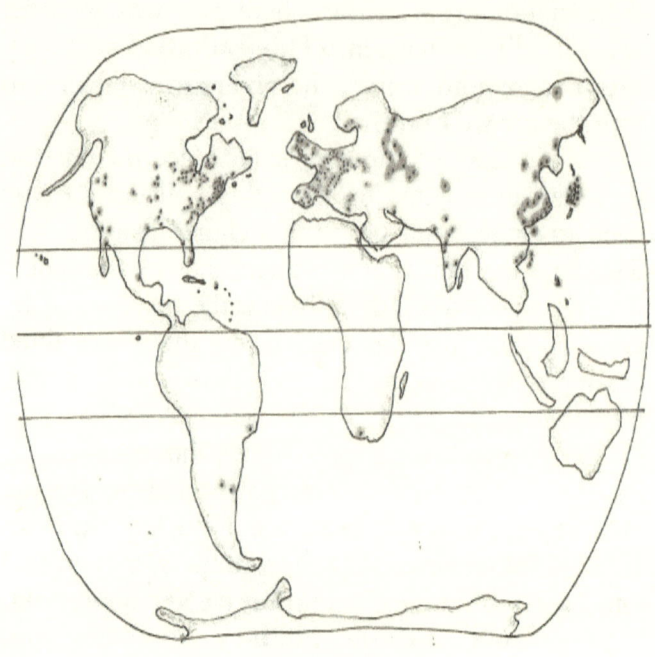

C-11 #1
Nuclear Power Dump Sites

Please note this map does not show dumping of radioactive material dumped into the oceans around the world.

Next you must understand just how the atmosphere of the earth works so as to understand how the distribution of radioactive material will unfold through the atmosphere.

Nature's Rights

The good part of mans use of earth air or the converting air into toxins, is that there is now less atmosphere. Less air equals less movement, which will help to temporarily localize the distribution to some degree. To understand air movement, one must take in to consideration all effects of the earth's movements. The following is my understanding of cause and effect of air and the spinning earth.

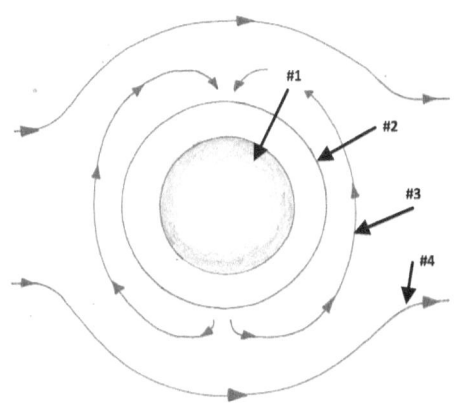

Image C-11 #2

Side view of planet showing air movement

Image C-11 #2

1. Earth
2. Air
3. Magnetic field protecting air
4. Sun's rays

This drawing shows the planet, (center) atmosphere, with the protective magnetic fields that keeps the air from blowing out into space, due to the sun's powerful rays as has happened to Mars. The magnetic field around earth permits life to have grown to such an abundant level that man can exist and destroy it. Without this magnetic field no air could accumulate and this would just be another dead planet like mars.

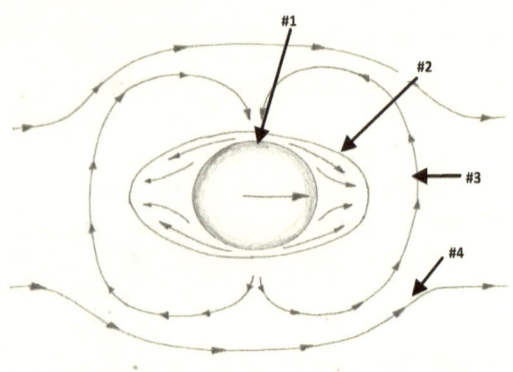

Image C-11 #3

1. Earth's rotation
2. Centrifugal force pushing air to the sides making it more dense
3. Magnetic field
4. Sun's rays or solar winds

Because the planet is spinning, its friction causes the atmosphere to become elliptical, making it thinner on the top and thicker on the sides.

As the air becomes denser, storms can grow too large in size, creating havoc upon the land.

When there is less air as there is now, there are less storms. This decrease in air via mans reckless consumption will be covered more intently.

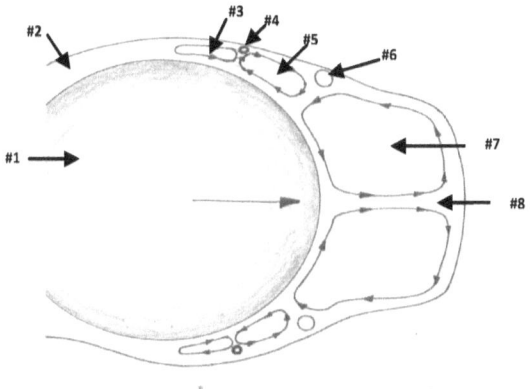

Image C- 11 #4 – Side view of Earth's atmosphere

1. Earth and its rotation
2. Air
3. North Pole, Polar Cell
4. North Polar Jet Stream
5. North Feral Cell
6. Northern Subtropical Jet Stream
7. Northern Hadley Cell
8. Equator
9. Southern Hadley Cell
10. Southern Subtropical Jet Stream
11. Southern Feral Cell
12. Southern Polar Jet Stream
13. Southern Polar Cell

The friction creates air currents that become tubes of circulating air and these tubes create the jet streams. These tubes of spinning air hold their shape for the most part, until heat and cooling effect their movement.

As is shown in this simplified view (image C-11 #4) of atmosphere circulation, the middle portion of the planet is split in half by the rotation of the sphere. The two Hadley Cells rotate in opposite directions from each other and lift the ever moving air upward, moving this air north and south and back down in the two major portion of the planet.

This will most likely contain the major portion of radiation spewing from these abandoned plants and land based abandoned dump sites, to the middle of the planet. The temporary safer zones would appear in this air current example to be found at the top and bottom of the world.

This land in the central part of the planet is where most of us live and is the reason this location was first on my list of concerns, but we rely on the oceans for much of our food. That is the second half of this part three of the 6th Die Off. To better understand this, the world inhabitants have for many decades been dumping radioactive waste into the oceans of the world with no regard to the eventual outcome.

The following is a map showing only the known oceans radioactive dump sites and the ones I know of that are not publicly reported on.

Image C-11 #5 Map of Ocean RADIOACTIVE Dump Sites

Hidden away in my archives is a map I have saved for decades that shows the Gulf of Mexico, outline of Florida and part of the Atlantic Ocean in fathoms. I have included this map because it shows government sanctioned dump sites the rest of us know little of. I have gone online and I have never found a copy of this map anywhere. To me it is disturbing as to the size of each of the designated unregulated dump sites. God only knows what is down there; I bet he doesn't even know it all. But Mother Nature knows and soon she will be

285

defending Nature's Rights in world court, dolling out punishment.

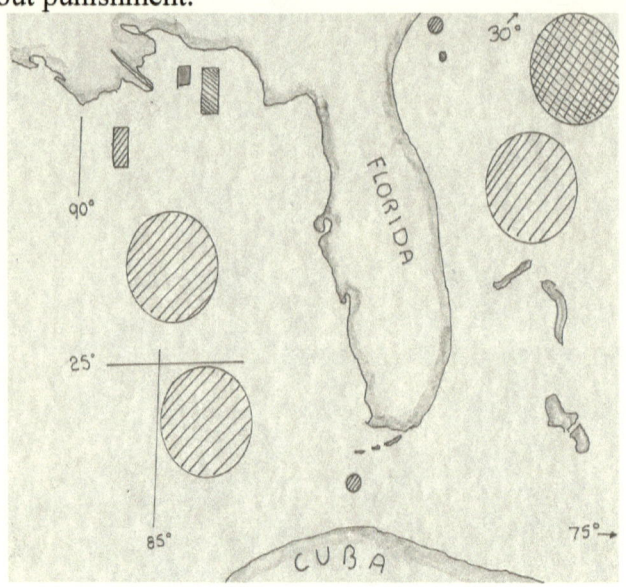

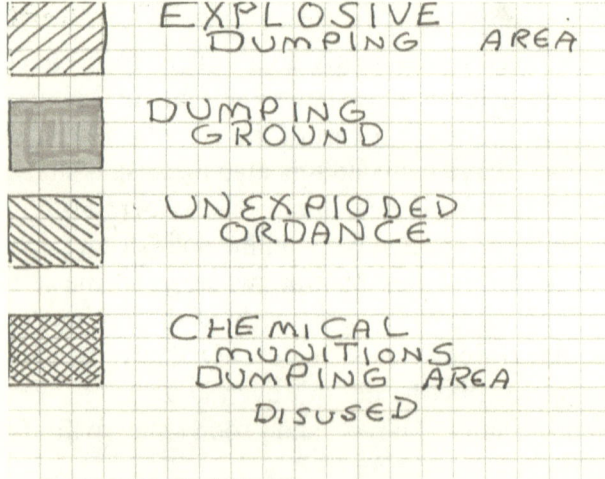

The reason for including this map is to show the disbeliever that the United States government would do this and has been doing this for a very long time. The dumping of cold war radioactive waste has also been detailed in recent news reports of the USS Calhoun County. Look up '**The Atomic Sailors'** and expand your mind as to the criminal element within the dark side of this secretive government and the future that is before us all in part three of the 6th Die Off.

The oceans have for a long time been the toilet of the world and due to its currents, some of the end results will be coming back at us in over the next thousand years. However, there is more than one type of ocean current and the next map shows the surface currents or warm water movements that will affect our near future.

Image C-11 #7 Warm Surface Currents

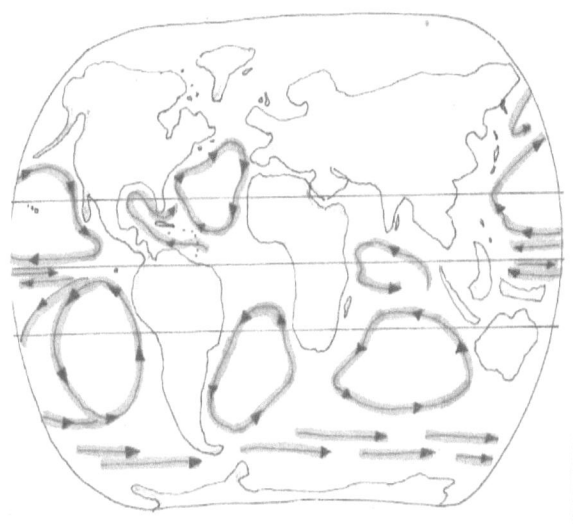

As we all know, heat rises and cold drops. This is true of oceans as well. The Great Ocean Conveyor Belt moves warm water to the north where it is cooled and then that water drops and is pulled under, circling the globe taking approximately 2000 years to re-emerge in some cases. The following map is to show the Ocean's Conveyor Belt.

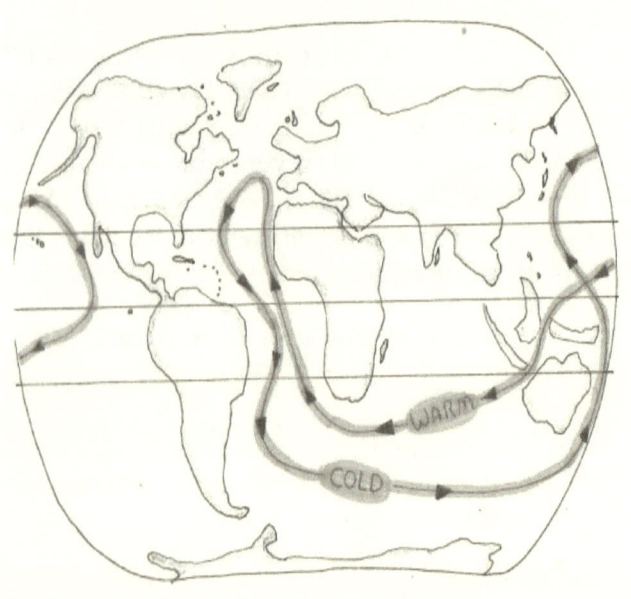

Image C-11 # 8 Map showing Present day Deep Ocean Conveyor Belt

Because radioactive waste will be with us for up to 5000 years, the surface and deep oceans will distribute their death to most parts of the planet. As the planet warms very quickly, these currents will change, because they are currently based on freezing poles on the north and south of the planet.

I predict as things heat up (and they will heat up very fast), massive highs will be created and become affixed over the largest oceans that are heating up. This will alter the shrinking air currents and jet streams as these large bodies of water heat up to new highs.

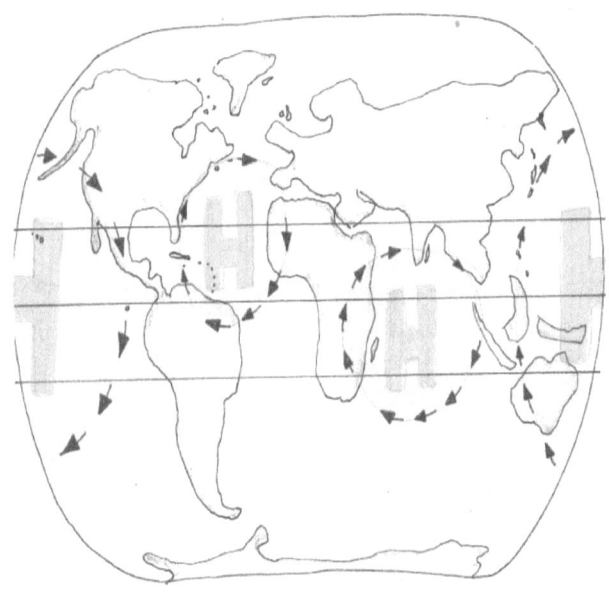

Image C-11 #9 Permanent Highs developing in the near future over the next 20 – 30 years

As the planet gets hotter and it will get much hotter without some type of major intervention, these highs will become stationary and remain over the super heated water. Life as we know it will become very hard and food very scarce, as life disappears. As time progresses, these highs will grow in size creating a massive heat zones encircling the earth.

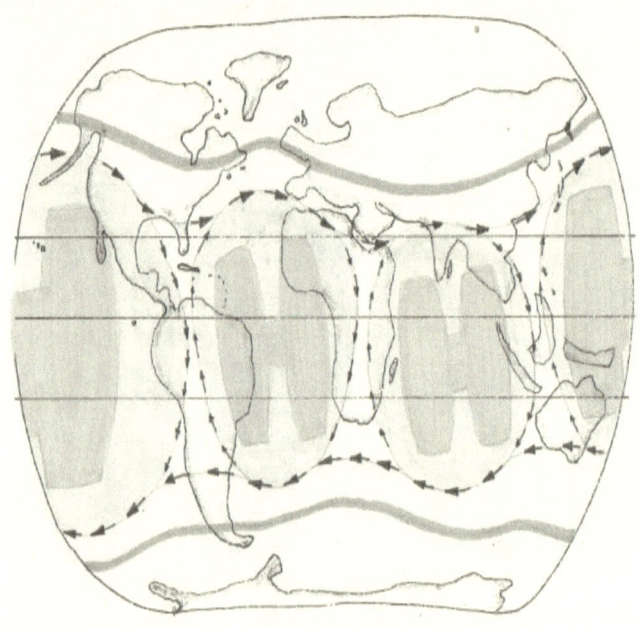

Image C-11 #10 Permanent Super Highs crossing the globe in the next 30 -50 years

The ever warming water will replace the cold water and it (cold water) will grind to a halt. Image C-11 #10 shows these super highs in place as the Great Ocean cooling Conveyor Belt grinds to a stop. All the polar ice caps will disappear in short order and costal cities will be submerged.

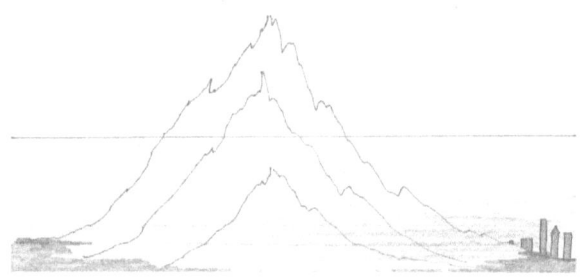

The only land available for man, not completed polluted, will be on the South Pole. The war for this last pristine area on earth will most likely ensue within the next 20 years and in the event to save man and his religion, this too will become destroyed.

Image C-11 #11 South Pole after all ice is melted

Nature's Rights

The long term effects of mans reckless endless consumption of air and replacing it with toxins will have a very long lasting effect. In such a short time, just about 100 years we have used up in my estimation up to 50% of our atmosphere.

Future generations will witness the long term effects of ignoring the warning signs for the greed of the all mighty **god/note**. The education of reckless consumption of such limited resources will be too late and have very long lasting consequences.

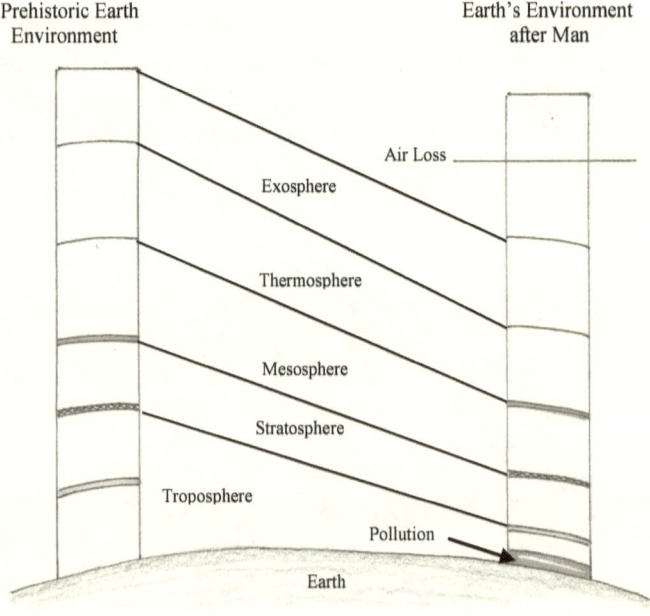

Image C-11 #12 Chart showing loss of air

Another clear example of the disappearance of Earth's atmosphere is found in the new mysterious cloud patterns supposedly mystifying the meteorologists. It is no mystery to me, because these straight line clouds are formed where the upper atmosphere is crashing down on the earth… is disappearing. I call these lines the **Consumption Line**. These lines are proof of mans endless consumption of the air we breathe to enrich themselves.

Image C-11 #13 Strata Consumption Line

As the aquifers disappear via our pulling this resource from under the ground, there is another effect that will be facing man and that will come in the form of a global disaster not yet consider by some. The water in the aquifers has a cooling effect upon the crust of the earth and when removing that water, we are removing the radiator that keeps the upper land cool.

As we permit the water to be removed from the aquifers, the earth's hot core can easily heat the thin crust and burn off the last of the water. One such example of this is the Ogallala Aquifer, where it is reported over 50% of this water is gone.

Equation: **The past 50 years of slowly disappearing Ogallala Aquifer, we've consumed 50%. The next 50% will take only 15 years, because pollution will destroy this source in less than 10 years.**

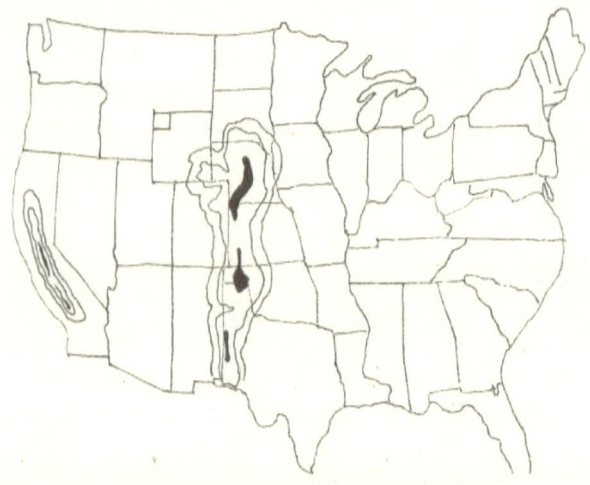

Image C-11 #14 The rapidly disappearing Ogallala Aquifer

At the rate we are removing this water and as the heat from the air and the inner core burn away the last of the water, we face a new disaster. History is about to repeat itself, once more the atmosphere of earth will most likely be plunged into darkness.

As it is believed that the Salton Sea was once a volcanic super eruption and it darkened the air for years. When we remove the cooling effects of the water from the ground the same thing is believed to happen.

The Yellowstone Park is where the Earth's core is trying to get to the surface. With mans help, (Global Warming, removing the aquifer) this may be in our future very soon. Intervention of a massive scale is required. I just don't see the people of earth doing the right thing and working together.

If we need to kill something, man is the one to call for; he is very good at that. But when it is time to save something, man is the last one to call.

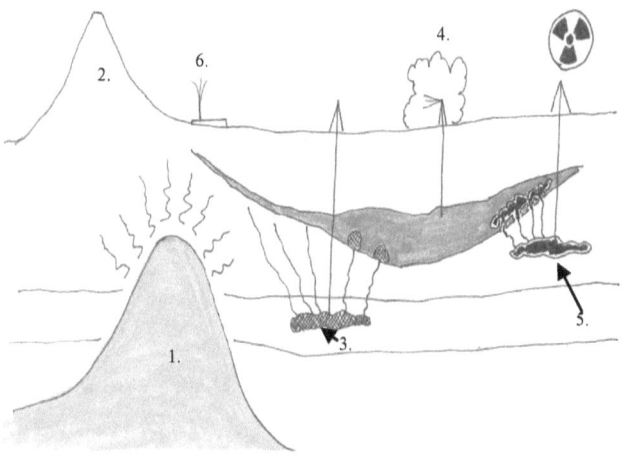

Image C-11 #15 Cut away showing Ogallala Aquifer

Nature's Rights

1. Earth's core coming to surface
2. Rocky Mountains
3. Fracking and dumping unregulated toxins into the earth.
4. Water removed from the aquifer and dumped onto the ground for food.
5. Radioactive material removed with chemicals now appearing in the drinking water.
6. Yellowstone National Park

Chapter Twelve

Summarization Of The Beginning Of
THE END

Sossusvlei Petrified Forest

Nature's Rights

It is because the majority of us possess a defective brain, that we are always looking for the quickest, fastest, easiest, laziest and cheapest way to accomplish any of the goals we set for ourselves in this very short life. This type of mind set sets you up to fail in attaining your goals, as well as if you come to everything with preconceived opinions. They block you from absorbing new and crucial information. I call this affliction The Tupperware Mind, nothing gets in and nothing comes out,,, it is sealed. You are set up to fail because you have all the answers. You have all the knowledge (even if it is wrong) and when you hear anything that conflicts with it,,, you dismiss it.

Example #1.) You have jumped to this part of the book,,, the ending,,, without reading the first part. Each chapter offers you, the reader, FOUNDATION for this part of the book. By your skipping over all the background, the foundation for each future conclusion, you set yourself up to fail. You most likely have been doing this all of your life.

Example 2.) You speed read everything,,, thereby missing much of the necessary information to help you. You take the time to buy a book for information and you skip over what you perceive as not necessary missing information. It is why you read a book a second time and get new information. The information was always there,,, but you skipped over it the first time. It is the reason a person giving a speech or a writer like myself,,, say or write things three times. First, I tell you what I am going to tell you,,, second I tell you what I wanted to say,,, third I talk about what I just said,,, three times. This is because of your defective brain and your constant need to THINK while READING prevents you from understanding.

These two examples are the reason you have jumped to the end the moment you bought the book. Knowing and recognizing this affliction will help you to absorb information from other people and stop interrupting them when they are telling you something or answering a question; like news reporter's do.

Knowing this now,,, I want you to stop, slow down and absorb the following information. For your sake I hope you read the previous pages of information. Your future,,, your families future will depend upon it.

Being able to look forward is not just a skill only humans possess, but many animals can see into the future. For us humans, it's not hard, just look to the past and you will see the future. The only thing is, there is no past like what lay ahead of us, so we can see the future clearly.

Therefore, much of the following is conjecture on my part and there are many variables that can divert mankind from the inevitable or what I predict will happen in the following conclusions. If it should be found that one of these conclusions is based upon false or erroneous information,,, all the other conclusions should not be tainted because of it.

It should be noted that the time to end the damage being done to this planet was in the late 70s and early 80s. We have passed the point of no return and now before us all is a horrific future unfolding that the millennium children must face.

Looking into the future is not easy, because there are so many variables that can alter the outcomes predicted. I tried to pull information from many angels to help acquire a time line. Each time line is based upon variables that only give an approximate time within the future of these events that are unfolding.

I have taken each event and its approximate time line and found the middle. Then added each date together and divided by the total and that is how I have come to the single date.

This date represents only the point in time when it will be abundantly clear that global warming is real. It is because of all the Deceivers on this planet,,, that it's too late to do anything (that I know of) to stop it from coming to its horrific conclusions.

If you approach the following information thinking it is pure science fiction; remember much of our present life is filled with future looking people that were motivated by science fiction writers. The list is long and I hope not necessary to write.

Each of the following dates will come with a Significant Factor (or SF #) from 0 to 100. I have rated each indicator of our future with a relevance value to show its significance. If the value is low, this indicator is showing only the course or direction we are all moving. A higher number will indicate the importance of that fact and suggest urgency.

1. Cheapest, fastest and easiest way comes through every part of our lives. The first indicator of the collapse of a society is for me, found within the traitorous government's Patent protection. Making the laws so complicated that every idea is rejected,,, Over working these people that review these application's only prevents a countries growth on new ideas. Sending our country's newest and brightest ideas, overseas to cheaper patent attorneys so as to save money, is literally giving away our future. The downward slide of this American industry is due to its complexity and cheapness. Its relevance is placed at a SF # of 15 and the date of the collapse is at or about **2021 to 2024**. Speed readers, if you need more information see page 42.

2. The premise that paper with ink on it as having value will show us all,,, as history

has shown us in the past,,, our belief in such a system will have a devastating effect upon every man, woman and child on this planet. Every government on earth relies on each of us trusting in a extremely failed system. Every country is going to face the same future as the inevitable collapse will bring down all nations. Its rating is very high, because when there is no money,,, people will stop flying in jet planes and Global Shading will end, causing supper heating. Currently (2017) the national debt is about to cross 20 trillion dollars and is predicted to cross the 24 trillion dollar line even quicker than first believed. As the dollar continues to drop in value this debt will grow faster. Therefore, I place the relevance number or SF # at 95 and predict the date to be **2022 to 2026**. For more information see page 57.

3. The consumption of air and turning it into a toxic gas is to have a very long term effect upon all creatures in the future. When there is no money, there will be no plane travel and the air, water and land will began to enter a phase of Super Heating. This will happen very fast after all airports are filled with planes that cannot fly, for there is no money to buy fuel. This factor is related to the one before (#2 money). I place a SF # of 98 and the time line is much the same as money, **2023 to 2027**. For more information see page 58.

4. In the near future,,, corporate America's goal of eliminating employees,,, will have a crushing effect on the economies (the dollar). When people cannot feed themselves or their families,,, the systems of governments will collapse. This will escalate the necessity of implementing Marshal Law and the FEMA Death Camps will open and start running at full speed. I rate the job disappearance with an SF # of 85 and the approximate date at **2023 to 2025,** when unemployment hits the 30 to 40 percent level. For more information see page 71.

5. The ocean temperatures have been rising at an alarming rate and the end result is a complete fish die off. There is nothing that is going to stop or drive down the inevitable outcome, which is ocean water will hit super heating levels. For a short time, nothing will survive, but a type of red or brown algae called, Phaeophyceae. No fish,,, no square sandwiches at our local fast food restaurants. As each source of food disappears, it will place strains upon the other foods. The point of no return has already passed and in the future, the loss of food (and greed) will drive up the prices. When the hunger of the masses becomes so strong it can no longer be contained, this will become an additional catalyst for the inevitable collapse. I place an SF # of 75 on this fact and a date of **2024 to 2028**. To learn more see page 104.

6. The loss of land in Louisiana is adding to the strain on our food sources. This is working within conjunction of the loss of food referred above. Less land to grow food drives up prices of the remaining food and the poor will not eat, driving up resentment. I therefore place the importance of this fact with a SF # of 60. I have given this a breaking point timeline at **2025** to **2030**. You can read more on this point on pages 112.

7. The Ogallala Aquifer is a large fresh water source that helps provide food to this nation and is soon to disappear. Removing water at this present rate will open up caverns that at a point will collapse (due to fracking), causing all this water to turn to mud. As covered in #'s 5 - 6, these strains will drive up food prices. I can foresee this water table resource becoming polluted with radiation and fracking toxins and place a SF # of 75. An approximate date of its disappearance is at **2026 to 2030**. To learn more see pages 139 and 195.

8. The destruction of the Black Sea is but brief example of just how destructive man is when looking at beauty and undisturbed wildlife. They find ways to exploit it. To be willing to do anything to have temporary riches and all the rest of us falling silently in line, shows just how ignorant we all are living within our defective brains. You see the life in the Black Sea is about to end for

good, from mans waste. This has an SF # of 10. The crash point will be in **2023 to 2025**. To read more see page 150.

9. The disappearance of the North Pole is very relevant in that it cools the air on the planet. When the ice goes and becomes tropical (for a short time) the center of the planet will become very hot and very desolate. This has a very high rating and will be one of the first indicators for man as to the end that I have been writing about. The final disappearance of this ice will see the start of the 6th die off. Therefore, I place an SF # 98 on this fact and this is when man will start to think; maybe Global Warming is real. The timeline fall in between the years of **2024 to 2026**. To discover more see pages 153 and 266.

10. I would never have thought I would see such a large and vast amount of life disappear in such a short time and without so much as a tear from man. The Great Barrier Reef can be seen from space and it was reported as of this year of 2017,,, 60% is dead. I give this a SF # of 98. Its end will be one place less that fish can spawn, feeding other fish that feed man. Its irreversible end will come between the years of **2021 to 2023**. See page 167.

11. Each example of the loss of food sources will only put a larger strain upon the remaining food. The rich will eat and the poor will starve. This, as of this year 2017

is happening and will only spread around the globe. Global starvation is at our doorstep and I place a SF # of 98 on this. The crash point will fall sooner than predicted by the experts, who are covering up the truth. I estimate the dates to be **2021 to 2023**. See page190.

12. This is another microcosm example of the ignorance of man to pursue the all mighty god/note as he strips and burns the Indonesia Rain Forest into non existence. This has a SF# of 60. Its crash point is **2024 to 2026**. See page 195.

13. The implication of the FEMA Death Camps will occur after Marshal Law is ordered. This will help slow the planets demise by removing human life on a vast scale not seen since the concentration camps of Hitler and Stalin's work camps (death camps) from the 1930s to the 1950s in the Soviet Union. See pages 203 and 218. *Anything that kills off the cause has no SF # and will only slow the inevitable outcome of the 6th die off before us all.*

14. Global warming will become Super Heating as the planet moves into this next stage, Nature's Rights. The host will do what it must to remove a parasite, like man does when he gets a fever to kill off a germ that has entered the body. The growing germ cannot live in the higher temperatures and when it is killed off (people), it lowers back to normal. Man is a parasite and will be

removed. This has a SN # of 85. See page 245.

15. The long range effects of the collapse of mans society will last thousands of years, until short lifetime breeding can build a resistance to radiation and still reproduce itself. This long term spread of radiation will encompass the globe to insure man will become extinct or have a vastly shorter lifespan. The death of long living man will have the same positive effect as the FEMA Death Camps. See page 272.

16. The very last I have chosen to relay to you is chart 7 on page 16 that reveals the greatest devastating indicator of the end of all life on earth, as we know it. At a point we will either give up and accept death and extinction of our species or we will rise to the challenge and face the carbon dioxide we are pumping into the air that is about to kill all life. All for those precious **god/notes**. This is the single greatest devastation facing man and is to be the final death nail in man's coffin on this earth. Unless we face the reality of its devastation and its part in perpetuating the 6th die off. If we as a being do nothing, the future outlined in this book is just ahead of us all.

The following is an approximate date in our near future, (derived from the above dates) that we will see the true beginnings of the 6th die off and its death knell ringing for us all to hear. It is clear this is going to happen and most all of us know it. We just cannot believe it will happen that soon,,, but it will!

1. **2021 to 2022.5**
2. **2022 to 2024**
3. **2023 to 2025**
4. **2023 to 2024**
5. **2024 to 2026**
6. **2025 to 2027.5**
7. **2026 to 2028**
8. **2023 to 2024**
9. **2024 to 2025**
10. **2021 to 2022**
11. **2021 to 2022**
12. **2024 to 2025**
13. **No number**
14. **No number**
15. **No number**
16. **No number**

> Add years together which equals 24,295 then divide by 12. Final date is
>
> 2024.5833

The final average date of the true beginning of the 6th die off started in the late 70s, when we all passed the point of no return chasing the almighty god/notes, under the watchful eye of the gods. The approximate date of the full devastating effects of a global die off, are ahead of us. I use all the indicating factors found in the book. Known to me to be true at this time, to ascertain the date to be,,,

Date range here

Since we have date ranges we add each column and divide each by 12 (number of dates per column) and this is the range you end up with

2023-2026

Add together and divide by 2

2024.5

Remember that these numbers are an approximation.

If you looked ahead (not reading the whole book) you wouldn't know how I logically arrived at these numbers.

Earth as the 6th Die Off unfolds

Nature's Rights

Dictionary
Terms and their hidden meanings

Al Qaeda: 1) a terrorist organization like Christianity, 2) an organization (like Isis) created in defense of Christian genocide.

American interests: 1) corporate greed, 2) a term given by the spin master to provide misinformation regarding large corporate financial investments, profits and/or gains, all guarded by young American blood, 3) big money, Dark money

Amnesty: 1) an act of desperation (by those in power), 2) to circumvent certain laws and render them invalid as needed to protect the powerful.

Anarchy: a result when laws are not enforced

Autodidacticism: autodidactism, autodidact, 1) self-directed learning, 2) self-education

Bad Ink: news reports of a negative nature.

Balance War: 1) a means to ensure the longevity of war to enhance profits, 2) opposite of quick and decisive.

Bankruptcy: a maneuver endorsed by the federal government, to gain profit for attorneys and other members of the legal justice system by using the financial misfortune of others. *Other countries use accountants to handle this,,, go figure.*

Bankster: 1) unprosecuted person within the banking industry that commits fraud or other criminal acts associated with lending, the mortgage trade, illegal commerce, stock exchanges, etc. 2) Persons who are above the law, 3) protected by Christians.

Big Three: The dominant group of three. (group automobile manufacturers.)

Blue Gold: Drinking water

Bribe: Political campaign contribution.

Change: A form of currency that gives the illusion of value

Chaos: The ever eroding pillar government sits upon to avoid the outcome of the future and what it helped to make.

Christian: 1) A religion stolen from the Jews whereby, they worship a bastard Jew executed criminal man 2) a religion that protects pedophiles at the highest level, the pope 3) a terrorist organization that permits killing across the globe

Citizen Terrorist: People that openly complain while working in the death camps.

CONOP 8888: Reportedly, an elaborate plan created by the U.S. Strategic Command (Pentagon) to counter an attack by an apocalypse zombie (the walking dead) outbreak.

Consumption Line: A straight line in the clouds indicating the disappearance of the Troposphere or the Stratosphere, where the Tropopause or the Ozone Layer that divide them is showing its collapsing division. Do to the conversion oxygen to toxic gas now mixing with the oceans.

COTE Calendar: Convergence of historical information providing predictable future outcomes.

D.D.D.: Drug Dealing Doctors.

D.O.O.M.: Devaluing Of Our Money

Dark money: A term given to **god/notes** that is untraceable and used to buy influence and power over other people in power.

Department of Disinformation: An elusive branch of the federal and state governments used to create and disseminate false statements and misleading information to the public.

Doomsday Clock: A time piece designed to predict the end of mankind via the Atomic Scientists.

Election Process: In America there is only one party (the rich) divided into two parts, Republican Democrat

Freedom Fighters: A term given to U.S. armed forces to justify invading other countries for their land, water or wealth.

God/note: 1) An illusion of safety 2) trick by those in power to give legitimacy 3) phony, fake, counterfeit, false, fraud, hoax, sham, etc.

Gods of Prey: Imaginary deities created by those wanting a free ride in life, taking advantage of the weak and frightened who are afraid to live, afraid to die.

GOTT MITUNS: German for 'God is with us' found on WWII belt buckles.

Goyim: 1) All people that are not Jewish 2) people considered by Jews as cattle 3) people of no value 4) people put on earth to serve the chosen ones

Greener Lands: Places filled with low intelligence people that the **BIG 3** take advantage of.

Inflation: A mythical explanation for the de-valuation of any paper currency resulting in higher prices and decreases in purchasing power

Insurance Fraud: Happens when you buy insurance and the carrier refuses to pay a claim.

Jew: A religion where only their people will go to heaven and the rest of us are Goyim not permitted in their land.

Mirror: 1) A place for the vain to relish themselves, 2) the worst invention man ever made

Moral Compass: 1) An ethical conscience that politicians do not possess, but pretend to. 2) a thing lacking in all religions

N.A.T.O.: Nations Access To Oil

Nicotine: 1) An addictive drug purchased freely without a prescription 2) an additive drug added to cigarettes to make them more addictive and profitable to the cigarette manufacturers (drug dealers) 3) a narcotic like cocaine sold freely with the blessings by Christian law makers

Occupiers: 1) Freedom fighters, 2) armies of domestic and foreign corporate criminals who take over and rule countries via their governments, 3) Christians

One Party: In Christian America the election system is but one party of the rich divided into two parts, the Republicans and the Democrats.

P.B. People: A natural occurrence in all species of life found primarily within ants called Polyergus Breviceps. Slave masters.

P.O.P.E.: Protector Of Pedophiles Everywhere

Persons of enemy of birth: Paranoid reaction to war permitting war crimes by a government against its own people.

Planned Obsolescence: A global business model that follows the premise of, "let's make all the cash we can now and let someone else pay to clean up the mess.

Plastic People: People of the plastic age of pollution, poisoning, and other destruction of the planet – modern man.

Poli-Christian: 1) An elected official that pretends to be a Christian for the purpose of getting elected and then violates the Christian values 2) the anti-Christ 3) type A personality of destruction.

Political system in America: A single governing body of the rich divided into two parts, Republican and Democrat

Politician: 1) Guardian of major corporations, 2) person willing to do anything for paper money

Religion and Ethics: A weekly news program on PBS that is allegedly an oxymoron.

Scrupulosity: 1) A psychological disorder 2) a madness that takes over the mind 3) an infectious mental delusion 4) mass hypnoses

Selection Process: Term describing the election process when large corporations buy (with campaign contributions) both sides of a ballot (all candidates)

Separation of church and state: 1) The First Amendment to the Constitution of the United States, 2) antiquated term used by Thomas Jefferson and atheists, 3) fallacy, 4) false premise and unforeseeable law, per the Christians.

Shark Market: 1) A place where you take your hard earned money, give it to strangers and they make fees off of you when they need cash 2) those who don't make money, but take money.

Simon Bar Legree: 1) A fictitious character made up by the writer of this book, 2) reprehensive, or representative of a real person unseen by the masses, 3) the darkest level of power any living human can obtain, 4) Satan that has tricked religious people to kill so he can control them.

Social Security Administration: The office that oversees the federal government's Ponzi scheme.

Speaking in tongues: 1) The art of speaking to God, 2) language of idiots, 3) created to fool the masses and take their money

Spin: Lies created to mislead and deceive the public.

String Master: 1) Title given to unseen corporate leaders (aka, puppeteers) who control elected employees, 2) mafia, an organization that, per the FBI, does not exist

Subsidies: Welfare for the rich.

Superior Body: 1) A governing organization that Christian America must report to, 2) a corrupt group of world leaders bought by the top 85 people in the world, 3) the United Nations or UN

Super Hyper-Devaluation: 1) A thing that happens to all paper money or god/notes, 2) often called high inflation however there is no such thing as inflation, 3) end result of a poorly run country usually for God 4) a people or race stripped clean by the **BIG 3** that know what they are doing.

White Gold: china from China

Nature's Rights

Books by William J Ryan

The Extermination of Kings, Part I
Journey to the Bay of Bengal - Revised

Two Tibetan monks witness the butchering and murder by the Chinese of all the inhabitants of a monastery in the Himalayas. As the only survivors and eyewitnesses, they face starvation as they are being hunted. They head south looking for sanctuary and are struck by the countless inhumanities they see and acts of destruction to the earth they love. *Available now*!

> ### *The Extermination of Kings, Part 1 – Screenplay*
> A version of the original book converted into a screenplay.

The Extermination of Kings, Part II
The Dark Continent

Word spreads of the only survivors and the monks receive help. Captain Jack, a big Irish seaman, gets them across the Indian Ocean and Osiris guides them across Africa through the perils they face there - man's inhumanity to man, foreign countries' trash and the consumption of all living things in order to survive. *Available Now!*

> ### *The Extermination of Kings, Part II – Screenplay* *Available!*

The Extermination of Kings, Part III
America

They are befriended by a billionaire that gets them to the land of the free but manipulates events for his own agenda. This is the last of the trilogy of easy to read fast-moving stories, with an outcome that helps the Tibetans gain power. *Available Now!*

The Extermination of Kings, Part III - Screenplay
A version of the original book converted into a screenplay.

Sheriff Jessy of Boonies, Kentucky 2007 Part I
An amusing and nostalgic look at an idyllic community and what happens when it is invaded by corrupt politicians. Sheriff Jessy tries to hold the community together in spite of black money and wins in the end. *Available now!*

> ### Sheriff Jessy of Boonies, Kentucky Screenplay
> A version of the original book converted into a screenplay.

Sheriff Jessy of Boonies, Kentucky 2009 Part II
Revenge of Dick and George, two boys from Texas
Politicians being what they are, bring an endless barrage of destruction to the community, with the goal of turning it into Lead Ville, USA. In their effort to destroy the community they expose Jessy and his dark secrets, with a tragic outcome. *Available soon!*

Levi's Reverse Wave Absorption
This is a riveting science fiction story about an Amish college student who invents a way to prevent earthquakes and pays for it with his life. As an FBI sting goes bad, corrupt Federal agents are exposed, taking you all the way to the top of the Government. *Available now!*

First Defense
Illegal drug trafficking across civilian lands, forces a community to defend themselves as the Federal Government looks the other way. *Warning: contains shocking solutions to real problems*, like Amy and her drill. *Available now!*

First Defense – Screenplay – *Available!*

The Good News Show
This is a scintillating scene by scene account of the news media, the control over the airwaves of American radio and television. With the unraveling of this empire comes a hard look at the future of our planet and the destruction that is coming. *Available now!*

The Good News Show - Screenplay *Available!*

Just Deserves
An in-depth look into life after death and the worlds beyond, from the vantage point of one who has just passed. Strange encounters and friendships develop as the earth reaches the end of its domination over man. *Available now!*

Just Deserves – Screenplay – *Available!*

The Copper Pit
A dramatic tale with an unlikely result of the President's and Congress's decision to banish outlawed street gangs to an abandoned copper mine in the middle of America's desert. *Available now!*

The Copper Pit – Screenplay – *Available!*

Seeds of Change
The story of a big city attorney who is forced by life events to move to a rural community which has been devastated by Federal Government programs like giving tax breaks to corporations that send American jobs overseas. A powerful political machine develops that changes the nation.
Available Now!

Screenplay *Available!*

Letters to President Obama, 52 weeks 52 letters

Here is actual White House correspondence (with responses) and commentaries written by a common small-town businessman struggling in the 2010 depression. It reveals the author's transformation from a confused and frustrated citizen, to an awakened and empowered one. *Available now!*

Car Slugs

This is a disturbing look into the retail car sales industry through the eyes of one mentally over stimulated salesman. The story is set in the heyday of the 1990's, before the destruction of our country by the banking industry. *Available Now!*

Car Slugs – Screenplay *Available!*

Scrupulosity Revised

Christianity is primarily used as examples of Scrupulosity levels One, Two, Three, and Four in this book, because of its power over this American government and its leaders, thereby all of us. The psychological disorder, Scrupulosity, is found by the author to be at a much more dangerous level than found in its classification, as a form of OCD (Obsessive compulsive disorder) for the author believes it manifests itself in the criminal behaviors of rape, murder, and genocide. There is a word describing these criminals of God and that word is Scrupulosity. *Available Now!*

Global Financial Super Heating

This is a dyslexic autodidacts' overview of most religions (afraid to live, afraid to die), resources, governments, their money, and the end of all life on earth if man continues to pretend that all is ok. The advantage of being an autodidact is that one is not encumbered with the knowledge of things taught, that one can or cannot do. It's all open for the author to share with you. With religions' blessings, the unregulated human population explosion is devastating this small planet and continues to leave only death and destruction as our legacies for future inhabitants. Lies from governments and religions and how 'The Big 3', controlled by the 85, are destroying the earth in pursuit of 'gods/notes' while the rest of us remain seemingly powerless. Right or wrong, are you prepared for what is to come? *Available now!*

In search for the "I"
My personal journey to understanding the complexities of all matter and the life it brings. From before the big bang to present day and back again. Life is a circle. How does the spirit of all life fit into all ordinary matter as we know it to be, beyond what we can see *The Complete Unified Circle Theory*. *Available Now!*

The Good Christian
A man finds a handwritten book amongst the belongings he found in a commercial storage shed he bought. This story takes you on two separate journeys of two different men that become intertwined by chance. One as a child that was raped by a priest suppresses the memories, and as an adult invokes vigilante justice. *Available now!*
> *The Good Christian – Screenplay –*
> *Available!*

Amaton Man – Ask a tree   for ages 6&Under
Available!
Amaton Man – The Secret for ages 7 to 12
Available!

Amaton Man – The Price for ages 12 to 18
Available!

Amaton Man – A Brief History
Available!

A series of coloring books meant to be used as a tool to aid in the fight against child sexual abuse. This coloring book is meant to help children, that have been or are being abused, to open up and tell someone, to empower them with the word, **"NO!"** in order to help them protect themselves. The stories within each of these books are meant for this purpose. *Available Now!*

The 3 Ks

A heart wrenching story based on a true double murder that happened in Tampa, Florida and the American Injustice System. Jon is a hardworking man trying to support his family and life a small portion of the American Dream. He comes home to find his wife and young daughter brutally murdered. After suffering the loss of his family, he is swept up in a life altering frame up that is perpetrated by blind and ruthless detectives in the Florida Justice System. The only thing that keeps him going is finding justice for his family and exposing the injustice that he had endured. *Available now!*

The 3 K's – Screenplay – *Available!*

Goyims

According to the Jewish religion, 98% of all people are not going to heaven and of the 2% that are going, they will go to heaven even if they don't believe in God. Regardless of your faith, regardless of your chosen god or gods, the outcome is the same; Armageddon. The faces of all man's Gods are but one and that is death in their names. *Available Now!*

Lords

Nature's Rights

A riveting drama about a historical religion fighting to reacquire its place in today's world, and love. The Lord King is a reincarnated God of the Aztecs, who fights to get back what once belonged to his people. Jan is a nurse who was once a tortured and abused child gets taken prisoner, but this prison is not at all what she expected. She finds peace from her past in an ancient ritual of freedom, and love. She is taken on a journey to a place she never believed she would see and finds herself as a Goddess. *Available Now!*

Lords – Screenplay *Available now!*

Dr. Ghee
This is a gripping science fiction story about a family that struggles to live with Alzheimer's disease. You won't believe what lengths that they will go as they work towards the day that they will find a cure for this debilitating disease and save future generations. *Available now!*

Dr. Ghee – Screenplay *Available now!*

Love and the Joy of Murder
A man and woman from seemingly opposite ends of society, find each other in the middle of a murder cover-up. This bazaar circumstance, narrated by the female victim, brings this unlikely pair together. They find that neither of them can or want to leave each other. From their closeness, love develops, as each of their personalities rub off on the other. They both have finally found joy, love and happiness in each other on the fringes of life and the law. *Available Now!*

Love and the Joy of Murder – Screenplay
This screenplay was entered into the **Hollywood Screenwriting Competition in**

2016 and was a finalist. **Placed 14th in the Action/Adventure feature category!**

Jesus Christ in Canaan

"Our race is the Master Race! We are divine gods on this planet. We are as different from the inferior races as they are from insects. In fact, compared to our race, other races are beasts and animals… cattle at best. Other races are considered as human excrement. Our destiny is to rule over the inferior races. Our earthly kingdom will be ruled by our leader with a rod of iron. The masses will lick our feet and serve us as our slaves"

These are just a few of the quotes that I have found that led me to investigate Jews and religion. I could not believe what I had found, so I wrote it down to pass it along to everyone. The stories within are true stories with some embellishment added to make them come alive to you, the reader. *Available Now!*

Dark Government

Beneath all governments are Dark Governments and their secretive networks to control and rule the world. This story is about what happens when the genetic growth of man is permitted to be altered and others move in to take control.   *Available now!*

Dark Government - Screenplay *Available!*

Grey Power – Project Term Limits

Have you ever thought about hurting someone that has hurt you, or thought about doing something to those in the government, because of the way that are running your country? If so, you need to read Grey Power ~ Project Term Limits.

When a world is on the brink of a catastrophic disaster and the people in power just don't want to take things seriously, what would you do?

Cooper has just retired from working at a bank and is very optimistic about his future. One day, everything changes and he becomes fed up with how those that are supposed to follow the rules persist on ignoring the rules that they don't like. He joins a very large group of people that have become fed up with how their country is being run, so they devise a plan to try to put things right. Cooper takes a trip that gives him a new lease on life in this harrowing tale of love, revenge, justice and peace at last. *Available now!*

Grey Power - Screenplay *Available!*

Aliens – What the hell is going on?

Life is not complicated, our defective split brains make this world full of riddles and we must rise above the confusion of our defective split brains.

Greedy people make things complicated to deliberately hide the truth. There is easy money to make for the few, if only a few know the truth. Knowledge is money and money is power and power can buy anything… like governments.

Today the rich flaunt their power over the rest of us in annual global meetings, showing off their religious symbols. Their power over us is unchallenged, because they own everything, including god and the future devastation as it's going on.

This book examines the hard facts of friendly aliens coming to earth over the past recent years. It is also of people behind governments that lie to their people to get the knowledge for new products of war that they can sell as their own invention.

Everything behind government is about power and money and the use of religion to control the masses. They will stop at nothing to keep control, power and money. It's just a big game to them.
Available now!

Nature's Rights

Adina of Elysium

Adina of Elysium is an historical story about two green children found wandering outside of a town called Woolpit in England. I wrote this story using the historical information that I found through my investigation.

In a place called Elysium, where there are no wars, the sun is low in the sky and the land is green all the time. Adina and her brother Mawukura were out moving their herd, when a force from above spooks them. It forces them and the herd into a dark cave, where they waited in confusion, for what spooked them to leave.

When they finally emerge from the cave, they find themselves in a foreign land. It's so bright that they could barely see what lay before them and so hot that Adina thought she would burn. When her eyes adjust a bit, she sees a dead barren land and assumes it's the land of death.

Our green children have to try to adjust to this land of death, for they don't know if they will ever find their way home again.

Available now!

Adina of Elysium - Screenplay *Available!*

An Amber Intervention

One man's taught hatred of other religions and race's of people is abruptly altered in a flash of light. He is forever changed by this event and becomes a different person.

In his attempts to help change the Earth and warn its people of the Intervention that is to come, he meets many who try to obstruct his message. With the help of his sister and an old flame that has come back into his life, as well as a new friend called Amaton Man, who is from a planet far away, he has some small success.

With or without Jim's help, this intervention is to come regardless of what the Deceivers tell people. Jim's goals are to expose the criminal element that has taken over. The animal lust to have it all at any price is exposed, to help in part, bring out the kinder side of mankind that is so rarely seen. *Available!*

Oh God! Not Another Murder

This book is a parodies' of the endless murder mysteries coming from the BBC, regarding a small village in England. Where after a series of these stories, one is forced to think... "They must have killed off every inhabitant of this village. Who would want to live in a place where the murder rate is higher than living in gang infested Chicago or the city of L.A.?

Each week we are witness to yet another murder. The religious leader interferes with the bumbling inspector that never gets it right and constantly resents the unwanted help. But ultimately, this man standing next to God can find the true killers. Maybe its his divine magical powers that only this religion has and is supported by the government for controlling (brainwashing) the masses. *Available!*

Deceivers

There is a secret organization that for hundreds of years have existed solely to obtain others land and riches by any means. War, murder, slavery, drug dealing and destruction of all other religions and their cultures are but a small part of the business models that they follow. To this day, these men hide behind governments and their corrupt politicians, moving freely, committing genocide for their chosen religion.

Most of these Deceivers embrace their god intensely for the sole purpose of enriching themselves. The few that truly believe in helping their fellow man are not advanced; they are removed or put to death. No one is to stand in their way.

Regardless of the pain, suffering and the extermination of those that stands in the way, their single goal is to control the slaves via religion and acquire wealth by any means possible. Rewriting history is easy when you own everything.

All those below the secret highest levels of this religious organization, inside as well as outside, are considered slaves. They are to do the bidding of the highest level people within this secretive cult. These "Lodges" around the world, enrich only the few while deceiving all others. This book exposes them; revealing their true agenda, money, wealth and power... using God.   *Available!*

Available now through Amazon.com and other fine retailers.